Dearest Betty-Lou

Art in Detroit
Public Places

Wishing you the happiest and healthiest of Birthdays!

We love you,

Ruth and David

Third Edition

Art in Detroit
Public Places

Text by Dennis Alan Nawrocki   Photographs by David Clements

DAVID CLEMENTS

With all best wishes,
Dennis Nawrocki

W

WAYNE STATE UNIVERSITY PRESS   DETROIT

© 2008 by Wayne State University Press, Detroit, Michigan 48201.
All rights reserved. No part of this book may be reproduced without
formal permission. Manufactured in the United States of America.
12 11 10 09 08   5 4 3 2 1

Library of Congress Cataloging-in-Publication Data

Nawrocki, Dennis Alan, 1939–
Art in Detroit public places / text by Dennis Alan Nawrocki ;
photographs by David Clements. — 3rd ed.
p. cm. — (Great Lakes books)
Includes index.
ISBN-13: 978-0-8143-3378-5 (pbk. : alk. paper)
ISBN-10: 0-8143-3378-8 (pbk. : alk. paper)
1. Public art—Michigan—Detroit—Guidebooks. I. Clements, David,
1948– II. Title.
N8845.D6N38 2008
709.774'34
2007045541

Designed and typeset by Maya Rhodes
Composed in Fournier MT, Zurich BT, and Agfa Waddy Ninety Seven
Maps created by Bill Nelson

Contents

NOTE ON PHOTOGRAPHY   VII

ACKNOWLEDGMENTS   IX

INTRODUCTION   XIII

A. DOWNTOWN DETROIT   3

B. CULTURAL CENTER   57

C. BELLE ISLE AND EAST   101

D. WEST AND SOUTH   131

E. MACOMB COUNTY   163

F. OAKLAND COUNTY   179

EPILOGUE   217

SUGGESTIONS FOR FURTHER READING   219

INDEX   223

Note on Photography

All text and cover photographs are by David Clements, except for the following:

A-2 by Herb Babcock
A-10 by Wyland
A-14 (p. 22), A-22 (p. 34) by Sergio De Giusti
A-22 (p. 33), A-36a–g by Balthazar Korab
B-22 by Wayne State University
D-23 by Andrea Blum
E-4 by Janice Trimpe
E-10 by Ray Katz
F-1 (p. 180, *top*) by Hartmut Austen
F-1 (p. 180, *center*) by Phaedra Robinson
F-1 (p. 180, *bottom;* p. 181, *top*) by Nick Sousanis
F-1 (p. 181, *bottom*) by Object Orange
F-7 by Dirk Bakker

Tri-Color Photographic, Royal Oak, Michigan, is responsible for all photographic processing and printing unless otherwise noted.

Acknowledgments

Art in Detroit Public Places could not have been realized without the enthusiastic support and participation of many individuals. That was as true in 1980 when the original edition of this book was published as it is now in 2008, twenty-eight years later. The idea for the first survey was proposed in the mid-1970s by Ann Woods, who, along with volunteers Liz Bank and Eve Cockburn, began to compile basic listings and visual documentation for a small guide to public artworks. They applied for and received a grant from the Michigan Council for the Arts (now Michigan Council for Arts and Cultural Affairs), which enabled them to engage Thomas J. Holleman, whose research and special interest in late nineteenth- and early twentieth-century Detroit history provides the basis for many of the discussions of pieces dating from those early years. The Detroit Institute of Arts' Founders Society and Department of Publications also helped make the 1980 edition a reality.

The impetus for the first revised edition (1999) occurred in 1994 with a grant from the Tannahill Faculty Enrichment Fund of the College for Creative Studies (CCS), which supported the initial groundwork for a new edition. The concurrent efforts of the national Save Outdoor Sculpture! (SOS!) cataloging of public sculptures in Michigan coincided with and influenced these first efforts.

Now, in 2008, SOS! and CCS have been again the mainstays in the production of this freshly expanded and revised text. Once more, I had recourse to SOS!'s exhaustive compilation of public art in southeastern Michigan from which to glean additional works of art for inclusion in the book.

And, true to form, my home institution, CCS, provided the critical infrastructural support through the summer and fall of 2006 and 2007 that such an organizational redesign of a book entails. With warm gratitude for their largesse, I thank Richard Rogers, Imre Molnar, Anne Beck, Mary McNichols, Julie Longo, Sandra Braden, Carlos Diaz, and my immensely patient and good-spirited office partner, Lisa Catani. Special thanks to Lindsay Hawkins, my computer-savvy helpmate through the summer of 2006. Unstinting support was provided as well by the CCS Library staff: Beth Walker, Mary Tobias, Nancy Steffes, Marian Lambers, and Robert Hyde.

Once the actual research and writing began, I was immeasurably aided by many gracious reference librarians and historians in the Detroit metropolitan area. In particular, I am obliged to Marianne Weldon, Jacob (Jack) E. Nyenhuis, and especially to Deborah Larsen, whose responses to numerous e-mail inquiries were invariably precise and informative. Art historians Linda Downs and Mary McNichols led me to heretofore undiscovered works, the latter sharing her original research with me. Daniel Redstone, architect, and Michael Davis of the Detroit Lions Academy furthered my research as well. My thanks also go to Ericka Alexander of the Detroit People Mover, Becky Hart at the Detroit Institute of Arts, and Sandra Schemske of the Wayne State University Art Collection for their ready assistance on various and sundry matters. I would also like to acknowledge Joyce LaBan and Grace Serra for their assistance in providing access to and information about the collections at William Beaumont Hospital and Detroit Receiving Hospital and University Health Center, respectively, which they have helped to form. Mark Coir and Brian Young of the Cranbrook Educational Community were hospitable hosts on my research forays to the school's campus. I was kindly updated by Darlene Carroll on the continuing *Billboard* project and by Keegan Mahoney on the developments in North Corktown.

Sincere gratitude is also extended to the many artists with whom I spoke about their works; they were unfailingly generous in sharing ideas about their art and sending along their résumés.

I also wish to recognize the usually unsung public relations and communications personnel at numerous institutions, facilities, and businesses who provided essential information or passed my inquiry along to those who could.

Nor were friends shy about providing suggestions and bringing works of art to my attention, including Lynne Avadenka, Rose De-Sloover, Barbara Heller, Ruth Rattner, Dolores S. Slowinski, Sergio De Giusti, and Giorgio Gikas. Sergio De Giusti, whose own art is included in this book, generously advocated the inclusion of the work of other artists, while conservator Giorgio Gikas readily and willingly responded to myriad inquiries from me on a wide range of matters both technical and aesthetic.

My dear friend and enthusiastic Detroit booster, Gary Eleinko, was my boon traveling companion as we logged countless miles crisscrossing the city to public art sites near and far in weather fair and foul. He, too, was not reticent in recommending this or that artwork, but the serendipitous discoveries we made on our journeys about the metropolitan area were unexpected and welcome dividends.

Kudos to David Clements, photographer extraordinaire and fellow appreciator of things Detroit, for the superb photographs that animate and deepen this survey.

I'd like to extend warm gratitude to Jane Hoehner at Wayne State University Press for her formative encouragement and shepherding both author and manuscript through the stages of publication. A debt is owed to Maya Rhodes for a fresh and handsome reinterpretation of this guide, and to Bill Nelson for his clear, comprehensible maps. Notably, as well, liberal appreciation is extended to copyeditor Jennifer Backer and production editor Carrie Downes Teefey, who smoothed out my grammatical infelicities while also mediating issues of content.

Affectionate salutations to my literary mentor, Susan F. Rossen, who first brought me into what became in effect a "lifelong" endeavor when, during that first summer, she broached a book that introduced me to the universe of public art and led to the first slim volume on Detroit's public art in 1980. Her steady and unwavering support during the gestation of all three editions lo these many years has been deeply sustaining.

Finally, boundless gratitude to my spiritual mentor, Magdalen Emeline Kaupa Nawrocki, who bolsters me to this day.

D. A. N.

Introduction

There has always been art in public places. Long before it was made for private consumption and enjoyment, art functioned for societies in basic and far-reaching ways. Religious beliefs have been a universal motivation behind works of art, with their power to inspire and to instruct worshipers in indoor and outdoor settings. The desire to immortalize after death has generated memorials ranging from the colossal pyramids of Egypt to the historiated steles or grave markers in countless cemeteries and the many kinds of memorials that grace an infinite variety of public spaces. The ability of art to propagandize, teach, and commemorate accounts for its frequent juxtaposition with government buildings, educational institutions, and public gathering places such as plazas and marketplaces. In such settings, works of art enjoy high visibility and accessibility. In addition to its power to influence, public art can also delight and extend viewers' enjoyment of their environment, thus combining the utilitarian with the aesthetic. For example, Roman fora, and their descendants, Italian piazzas, which function as vital communal centers, are replete with statues, fountains, and monuments of every kind and description.

American cities have also created a legacy of art, celebrating their own histories and heroes. Detroit and its environs are filled with examples linking us to the time-honored traditions outlined above. The city's older cemeteries, Elmwood and Woodlawn in particular, are rich in examples of funerary art dating back to the late nineteenth century (C-6, D-9). Scattered in downtown squares and inner-city parks are numerous memorials to important figures in the history of Detroit and Michigan, such as General Alexander Macomb, Stevens T. Mason, Hazen S. Pingree, Father Gabriel Richard, and Alpheus Starkey Williams (A-34, A-4, A-6, C-9, C-15). The city also boasts a host of sculptures relating to government buildings: the late nineteenth-century sculptural group of *Victory and Progress* is a prominent feature of the Wayne County Building, and *The Spirit of Detroit* (A-16, A-24) is a major element of Detroit's "city hall," the Coleman A. Young Municipal Center. A group of historical figures by Detroit's first sculptor, Julius Melchers, which once were exhibited in the niches of the old city hall, have been reinstalled in a plaza setting at Wayne State University (B-17).

The desire of Detroit's early citizens to develop an extensive public park system was accomplished and enriched by the construction of many fountains and monuments, particularly on Belle Isle (C-10–18), the city's most spectacular park. Libraries and schools have also encouraged the public display of works of art, celebrating the connections between artistic creations and centers of learning. Most outstanding in the Detroit area is the extensive collection of outdoor sculptures on the 315-acre grounds of the Cranbrook Educational Community (F-14–19) in Bloomfield Hills, the majority by the renowned Swedish sculptor Carl Milles.

Unfortunately many American cities have destroyed, neglected, or been indifferent to their architectural and artistic heritage. Urban sprawl and the development of suburban satellites have too often resulted in destruction and deterioration with the result that many important buildings and monuments all across the land have been lost forever. It is the intent of this book to point out the many striking and important instances of public art from Detroit's past that still exist, as well as to show that the precious tradition of art in public places is indeed alive and flourishing in this city and its surroundings.

Within metropolitan Detroit, the presence in public areas of numerous works of art by such important national and international figures as Gutzon Borglum, Alexander Calder, Sam Gilliam, Robert Graham, Isamu Noguchi, Carl Milles, and Louise Nevelson, alongside fine pieces by many noteworthy area artists, is a rich heritage indeed. It is my hope that by featuring a selection of works, old and new, this book will help us understand better what we have, must keep and protect, as well as encourage in the way of public art. Whether financed by public monies or private bequests, intended to aggrandize the memory of a private citizen or to provide benefit for the general public, the works gathered here are valuable ties to our past and honest, incisive statements about our present and future.

The riots of 1967, perhaps more than anything else in recent Detroit history, made clear the jeopardy in which Detroiters, through neglect, had placed the city and its art. In the wake of these upheavals, four decades of on-and-off-again renewal have yielded noteworthy results. A revitalization is underway not only in downtown Detroit but in the city's neighborhoods as well. Funding for these diverse projects has come from both public and private sources. Detroit Renaissance, an organization of the chief executives of the area's leading corporations, and New Detroit, Inc., a coalition of civic leaders, sponsored a series of sculptures and murals (A-12, C-11, C-20, D-6) in downtown and neighborhood sites. In addition, the City of Detroit Recreation Department has been and continues to be an energetic patron of public art, funding artwork for parks throughout the city (A-11, B-2, D-8, D-14). More recently, Detroit 300, a nonprofit organization formed as the city approached the tercentenary of its founding in 2001, spearheaded not only the reconfiguration of Campus Martius, the historic core of the Motor City, but new monuments as well (A-2, A-21). And the Greater Corktown Development Corporation has enhanced the rejuvenation of an inner-city neighborhood with pocket parks and public art (D-4).

The generous bequest of Mrs. Horace E. Dodge made possible Noguchi's futuristic fountain in Hart Plaza, continuing the tradition embodied in such older works as the Scott, Barbour, and Rackham fountains (C-10, C-12, F-2) of a private individual creating a monument for public benefit. The patronage of Lila and Gilbert B. Silverman (A-33, B-24, C-2), Margo V. Cohen (F-19), and Frederick and Barbara Erb (F-20) represents recent instances of civic philanthropy. Hospitals have also become liberal patrons, as seen in the expansive collection of Detroit Receiving Hospital and University Health Center in the Medical Center, as well as in the burgeoning holdings of William Beaumont Hospital in suburban Royal Oak.

Corporations both within and beyond the city limits have also taken the lead in supporting public art; among distinguished corporate commissions are the Manzu dancer poised at the entrance to the One Woodward Plaza building, the Calder stabile formerly installed in front of the AT&T Building, and the spiky Surls sculpture dominating the façade of Neiman Marcus (A-25, B-8, F-10). Notable as well are the several works that embellish the exterior of the Blue Cross Blue Shield of Michigan complex (A-14, A-15). The developers of a number of huge shopping centers have commissioned many monumental works of art to decorate these vast commercial environments (D-21, D-22, E-8). Indeed, our shopping malls have become public gathering places, ensuring works of art displayed in their midst a steady stream of observers.

Artworks have enlivened many public spaces in the city in the last two decades. Each of the thirteen People Mover stations is enhanced with a two- or three-dimensional work (A-36a–g), just as the riverfront parks have been complemented with both site-specific installations and individual works (C-1). Also noteworthy, albeit not featured in this book, are the numerous benches designed for the Boll Family YMCA by a host of artists and designers, including Lois Teicher, Mark Beltchenko, and Gary Kulak, among others (B-9, D-10, E-5). Provocative, colorful wall paintings have surfaced of late as well (B-12, D-1, D-3). A flourishing muralistic practice in Mexicantown is especially noteworthy (D-12, D-13). The Art in Public Places program inaugurated in 1999 by Mt. Clemens represents another emphatic acknowledgment that public art can strikingly transform modest and familiar city spaces (E-5, E-6).

As we move forward in the twenty-first century, metropolitan Detroit is a municipality in process and transformation, with much current building, from sports centers and gambling casinos in the city to suburban civic campuses and renovated pedestrian-scaled, vintage "downtowns." Consequently, additional works will be designed for and installed in public spaces in the future, especially as the area's multiple city centers are renewed and revitalized. Some communities have begun experimenting with the temporary siting of sculptures to invigorate public spaces; in both Birmingham and Sterling Heights, for example, initiatives are in place that involve paying stipends to artists for the loan of their work for a specified length of time. At the conclusion of the two- or three-year contracts, the pieces are removed and a new roster of artists is invited to install artwork. Interestingly, at the same time that contemporary projects are realized, older sculptures are often resited to their advantage, the change of venue providing spectators with a fresh and novel point of view (A-1, A-6, A-7, A-11, B-8). In suburban Troy, the relocation of Michael Ayrton's colossal *Head* from a commercial to pastoral setting has yielded fresh insights into the work (F-11).

Arguably, the most dramatic expansion of the universe of public art in the opening years of the new century was the creation of the Josephine F. Ford Sculpture Garden in the heart of Detroit's Cultural Center in 2005 (B-10, B-11). Housing ten major examples of post–World War II sculpture on a two-acre quadrangle of lawn and trees plus one early twentieth-century work, it is the first public sculpture park in the metropolitan area. With funding provided by Mrs. Ford, coupled with the exemplary collaboration between the College for Creative Studies (which provided the real estate) and the Detroit Institute of Arts (which loaned the art), the city's aesthetic capital was persuasively augmented in one fell swoop.

Amid all this constructive change, however, there continue to be losses—wall paintings flake and fade, sculptures rust and are graffitied. A persistent deficiency in Detroit and other cities is the lack of ongoing maintenance for public art. Often what goes up in a glare of publicity deteriorates with scarcely a backward glance. Yet watchful preservation groups like Detroit's Friends of Belle Isle and the national SOS! (Save Outdoor Sculpture), a jointly sponsored program, founded in 1992, of the National Museum of American Art (Smithsonian Institution) and the National Institute for the Conservation of Cultural Property, are decidedly encouraging.

Significant losses have occurred in the intervening years since the 1999 edition of this book: the mural by John Egner on the rear wall of the Park Shelton Apartments building in midtown was partially obliterated by new construction; the playscape by Vito Acconci formerly located in St. Aubin Park along the riverfront was demolished; and the shimmering construction by Richard Lippold suspended from the ceiling of the Fairlane Town Center in suburban Dearborn was de-installed pending conservation. Equally alarming is that as of this writing, John Chamberlain's *Deliquescence* (A-32) has not yet been returned to its McNamara Federal Building site since its removal for restoration in 2005.

Nevertheless, there is so much art in public places to be found in southeastern Michigan, and it is of such immense variety, that I had to limit my survey to objects located within a twenty-mile radius of downtown Detroit. The works included are found mostly, but not exclusively, outdoors—in parks, plazas, and squares, on the exteriors of buildings, and in courtyards. Buildings or institutions that

I have defined as public in nature encompass government offices, libraries, shopping centers, hotels, banks, hospitals, universities, and colleges—but I have restricted my choices to works on view in publicly accessible interior spaces.

Since 1980, the date of the first edition of this book, approximately one hundred new examples have swelled the corpus of public artworks in the Detroit metropolitan area. The 1999 edition of this guide grew from eighty to one hundred twenty objects and/or sites. For the present edition, we have maintained the pace, adding thirty-six entries (and deleting seven) although fewer years have passed between editions. Not surprisingly then, this publication has grown not only in physical size but also in breadth. To be sure, though we have included a plethora of recent works (A-9, A-22, F-13), an equal number of pieces heretofore overlooked (both old and new) have been incorporated (for example, C-7, D-23, E-7, F-4). In short, more has been added than taken away. Significantly, this increase in numbers has broadened and deepened the comprehensiveness of the text, attesting to the enduring life and growth of a place too often portrayed as a declining metropolis. Indeed, a book such as this can never be definitive but will always be provisional; the next edition, when published, will undoubtedly wax or wane as the saga of public art in Detroit, as in any vital city for that matter, advances, retreats, and then charges forward once more in the course of its singular history.

This book is organized into six geographical districts, each introduced by a map to facilitate a walking or automobile tour of the included works. The 149 entries—several of which cover multiple objects (such as A-36a–g, B-4, and F-1)—I have chosen to highlight with an illustration and accompanying text were elected on the basis of quality, historical interest, variety of types and media, and geographic distribution. Each discussion includes a brief history of the piece—where, when, and by whom it was created—as well as the nature of the commission. We have also tried to place each object within its art-historical context, suggest the artist's intentions, and discuss the relationship of the artwork to its location.

In the initial research for this publication in the late 1970s, volunteers at the Detroit Institute of Arts compiled a comprehensive list of public artworks in the greater metropolitan Detroit area. This checklist, approximately 300 entries in length, has been added to in the years since that original documentation and now numbers over 400 examples, attesting to the vast array of public art in our midst. This surprising number, in a city that is often and mistakenly stereotyped as only capable of making automobiles, forces one to reevaluate the actual character of Detroit. As is true of any modern urban complex, one has to look beneath surfaces for the true character of a place. Although Detroit seems to have been more interested in its future than its past, and perhaps at times even more cavalier in its treatment of history than other cities, it does in fact possess many observable traditions, including that of public art. This book, then, celebrates the variety and vitality, toughness and sensitivity, and past and future of the artistic legacy of this great city.

Detroit Metropolitan Area

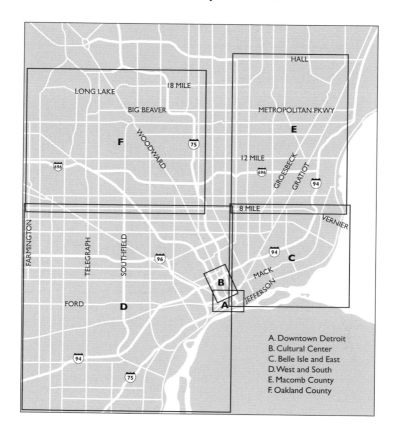

A. Downtown Detroit
B. Cultural Center
C. Belle Isle and East
D. West and South
E. Macomb County
F. Oakland County

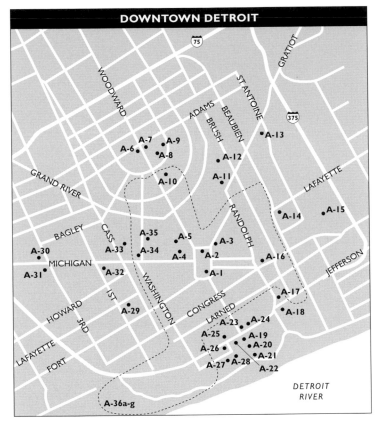

DOWNTOWN DETROIT

A-1. Michigan Soldiers and Sailors Monument
A-2. Monroe Monument Marker, Woodward Monument Marker
A-3. Abraham Lincoln
A-4. Stevens T. Mason
A-5. Sentinel X
A-6. Hazen S. Pingree Memorial
A-7. William Cotter Maybury Monument
A-8. Russell A. Alger Memorial Fountain
A-9. Millennium Bell
A-10. Whale Tower
A-11. The Entrance
A-12. Hard Edge Soft Edge
A-13. The Hand of God, Memorial to Frank Murphy
A-14. Dancing Hands, Urban Stele
A-15. The Procession (A Family)
A-16. Victory and Progress
A-17. Christopher Columbus
A-18. George Washington

A-19. Pylon
A-20. Horace E. Dodge and Son Memorial Fountain
A-21. International Memorial to the Underground Railroad
A-22. Transcending
A-23. Memorial to Joe Louis
A-24. The Spirit of Detroit
A-25. Passo di danza (Dance Step)
A-26. Gomidas
A-27. Victory Eagle and Pylons
A-28. Abraham Lincoln
A-29. Untitled
A-30. General Thaddeus Kosciuszko
A-31. Kevin C. Flaherty Memorial
A-32. Deliquescence
A-33. Wish Tree for Detroit
A-34. General Alexander Macomb
A-35. Color Cubes
A-36a–g. Art in the Stations

A. Downtown Detroit

A-1
Michigan Soldiers and Sailors Monument
Randolph Rogers (1825–1892)
Campus Martius Park, Southern End
1867 (dedicated 1872)
Bronze and granite

This imposing monument is one of America's first Civil War memorials and among the oldest examples of public art in Detroit. The commission was awarded to Randolph Rogers, a native of Ann Arbor, Michigan, on the basis of a competition held in 1867. Like many American sculptors of his time, Rogers was drawn to Italy, where he lived from 1848 until his death. Typical of memorials created in the wake of the Civil War by Rogers and his contemporaries, the monument is organized in an octagonal grouping of symbolic statues arranged on four levels. Steps lead to the main platform, where four fierce eagles with gaping beaks and outspread wings stand guard on pedestals. Between them are four seven-foot military figures representing Artillery, Cavalry, Infantry, and Navy, separated by relief portraits of Lincoln, Grant, Sherman, and Farragut. Seated on the next level is a quartet of females personifying Victory, Union, History, and Emancipation (the latter may represent slave liberator Sojourner Truth). When the memorial was dedicated in 1872, the female figures had not yet been completed; they were installed in the 1880s.

The monument is crowned by an eleven-foot allegorical representation of Michigan, a robust and powerful female warrior wearing a winged helmet, holding aloft a shield, and brandishing a sword. Directly underneath the figure a bronze tablet reads: "Erected by the people of Michigan in honor of the martyrs who fell and the heroes who fought in defence [sic] of liberty and union." The vigorous stance and aggressive character of Rogers's image provide a striking contrast to the more fluid, graceful interpretation of the same subject by Daniel Chester French (A-8).

The memorial's granite base and figures were moved 125 feet south of its original site when Campus Martius and adjoining streets were reconfigured in 2003. At the same time, the stepped stone edifice was remounted on a dark granite base—animated by four projecting fountains—which increased the monument's sixty-foot height by approximately five feet. The resiting also brought this oldest of monuments into dramatic alignment with the sleek, modernistic *Pylon* by Isamu Noguchi three blocks south at Woodward and Jefferson (A-19). Rogers executed a commemorative ensemble very similar to Detroit's for Providence, Rhode Island.

A-2
Monroe Monument Marker
Woodward Monument Marker
Herb Babcock (b. 1946)
Eric Ernstberger (b. 1955)
Campus Martius Park, Northern End
2003–2004
Glass, stainless steel, granite, electric light

Two twenty-two-foot-tall stainless steel towers mark the northern end of Campus Martius in the middle of downtown Detroit. Their designer, Indiana-based Eric Ernstberger, conceived of them as illuminated beacons that designate a significant location or public destination. In fact, on special occasions, a flame can be kindled in the sizable shallow "bowl" at the top of each. Ohioborn Herb Babcock, longtime professor of glassmaking at the College for Creative Studies, designed and fabricated the twenty-one cast-glass panels that his colleague's columnar armatures support. *Monroe Monument Marker* (2003) (*opposite*), sponsored by DTE Energy, is dedicated to the city's cultural life. The imagery of its nine panels (staccato arrays of dots, bars, lozenges, and radiating diagonals) symbolizes music, art, performance, design, and architecture. *Woodward Monument Marker* (2004) (*this page*), financed by Lear Industries, commemorates Detroit's industrial ethos. Abstracted images of wheels, tools, and cones visible on its twelve glass segments allude to research, technology, manufacturing, and transport.

Funded, developed, and endowed by the Detroit 300 Conservancy to celebrate the founding of Detroit in 1701, Campus Martius, with its fountains, gardens, performance stage, seasonal ice-skating rink, and newly minted and historic public art, including the *Soldiers and Sailors Monument* (A-1), constitutes a spirited and vigorous nucleus for a city over three hundred years old.

A-3
Abraham Lincoln
Alfonso Pelzer (d. 1904)
Library Park, Library and Farmer Streets
1898 (fabricated c. 1915; replica cast 1999)
Bronze and limestone

The original of this statue was first presented to Henry N. Leland, president of Lincoln Motor Company, and for years stood in front of the company headquarters at West Warren and Livernois avenues. In 1958, after the company moved to a new location, Leland's son gave the statue to the city. Fabricated about 1915, Detroit's *Abraham Lincoln* was one of six replicas of a sculpture designed by Alfonso Pelzer of Salem, Ohio, for Lincoln, New Jersey. It was made of two-ounce sheet bronze and assembled in sections, a method less expensive than casting. Located in a small, leafy, semi-enclosed park behind the downtown branch of the Detroit Public Library, the statue was badly vandalized in 1997. A replica in cast bronze has been mounted in its place, and the original, its vulnerable surface now restored, has been set up in the library's main building on Woodward Avenue.

The slightly smaller-than-life-size Lincoln is shown with his left hand holding the partially unrolled *Emancipation Proclamation* and his right hand opened in a welcoming gesture, emphasizing his historical significance and the generosity of his character. The simple pedestal contains the incised words "Let Man Be Free."

German-born Pelzer arrived in the United States in the early 1890s and worked assiduously as a sculptor in Salem during that decade, returning to Germany around the turn of the century. The four large figures representing Law, Commerce, Agriculture, and Mechanics atop the Wayne County Building (see A-16) are also attributed to Pelzer. Other works by this artist are in Indianapolis, Peoria, Boise, and suburban Pittsburgh.

A-4
Stevens T. Mason
Albert Weinert (1863–1948)
Capitol Park, Griswold Avenue
and State Street
1908
Bronze and granite

This monument stands on the site of the state's first capitol building. In 1831, at the age of nineteen, Stevens T. Mason (1811–1843) was appointed secretary of the Territory of Michigan by President Andrew Jackson. Although Mason was young and politically inexperienced, he led the successful petitioning of Congress to declare Michigan a state and served as its first governor from 1836 to 1840. His ashes were reinterred in 1905 at the site of this monument, which was unveiled in 1908. Sculptor Albert Weinert was born in Germany and studied at the Ecole des Beaux-Arts, Brussels, before settling in the United States. He depicted Mason as a young statesman standing confidently on a pedestal representing in relief two fasces, bundles of sticks bound with a double-headed ax, Roman symbols for the power of magistrates. A semicircular platform and balustrade once surrounded the pedestal and statue, like the *James J. Brady Memorial* on Belle Isle (C-14); they have been demolished.

A-5
Sentinel X
Morris Brose (1914–2000)
Capitol Park, Griswold Avenue
and State Street
1979
Steel

Morris Brose's dark, commanding *Sentinel X* still towers above the ever-encroaching trees planted at the time of its installation in Capitol Park in 1979. The slender, ten-foot-tall *Sentinel* is one of a number of sculptures based on this theme begun by Brose in 1968. These solitary, upright personages, whose stances echo the erect posture of the human body, have been realized in wood, bronze, and here in steel. All are topped by jutting forms that suggest arms or a head, as if, alert and watchful, they protect and witness all that transpires around them. A notable feature of *Sentinel X* is the long, swelling curve at left that contrasts dramatically with the sculpture's angular silhouette and subtly implies the rounded profile of a human torso. Brose's *Sentinel* shares the small, downtown Capitol Park with the statue of Governor Stevens T. Mason (A-4), thereby creating for the visitor a lively dialogue between a figurative and nonfigurative artistic vision.

Born in Poland, Brose emigrated to the United States and arrived in Detroit in 1931. Although well established as a successful businessman by the 1940s, he gave up that career in 1949 to study and make art. Brose's sculpture is well represented in the Detroit area, including another composition from the sentinel series, *Sentinel II* (1968), on the campus of Wayne State University.

THE CITIZENS OF MICHIGAN
ERECT THIS MONUMENT TO THE CHERISHED MEMORY OF
HAZEN S. PINGREE
A GALLANT SOLDIER
AN ENTERPRISING AND SUCCESSFUL CITIZEN
FOUR TIMES ELECTED MAYOR OF DETROIT,
TWICE GOVERNOR OF MICHIGAN.
HE WAS THE FIRST TO WARN THE PEOPLE OF THE GREAT DANGER
THREATENED BY PRIVATE CORPORATIONS AND THE FIRST TO
ARISE STRONG ENOUGH TO INTERPOSE THE POWER OF
THE PEOPLE TO STEM THE TIDE
THE IDOL OF THE PEOPLE
HE WAS BORN IN MDCCCXL AGED 60 YEARS

A-6

Hazen S. Pingree Memorial

Rudolph Schwarz
(1856–1912)
Grand Circus Park,
Western Half,
Woodward Avenue and
West Adams Street
1903
Bronze and granite

A great populist reformer, Hazen Pingree (1840–1901) was twice elected governor of Michigan and four times mayor of Detroit. The plaque on the pedestal lauds him as "The Idol of the People" and lists "The Citizens of Michigan" as the donors of the memorial. Sculptor Rudolph Schwarz, born in Vienna, emigrated to the United States, where he established a respected sculptural practice by the time of his death in Indianapolis in 1912. Schwarz, who won the competition for the Pingree statue in 1902, interpreted Pingree as a caring and responsive man. He is depicted turning his body and directing his gaze to the right, toward something that has demanded his attention. His credibility as a man of the people is further reinforced by the simple fringed parlor chair in which he sits. Mounted on a high, stepped pedestal, the commanding bulk of Pingree is framed dramatically by a backdrop of trees and sky. In a 1997 relocation of the Pingree and Maybury statues (A-7), these longtime political opponents now collegially face pedestrians and motorists traveling south on Woodward Avenue.

A-7
William Cotter
Maybury Monument
Adolph Alexander Weinman
(1870–1952)
Grand Circus Park, Eastern Half,
Woodward Avenue and East
Adams Street
1912
Bronze, marble, and granite

This formal, classical monument is dedicated to William Cotter Maybury, who served both as city attorney (1876–1880) and mayor of Detroit (1887–1905). The designer, Adolph Alexander Weinman, was born in Germany, came to the United States when he was ten, trained with prominent sculptors Daniel Chester French (see A-8) and Augustus Saint-Gaudens, and then commenced a productive and prolific sculptural career in North America. He is represented in Detroit by two works, the General Alexander Macomb memorial (A-34) and this one.

In this example of his style, Weinman depicts Maybury, in a decidedly informal pose, seated in a stately, fringed chair. The mayor's jacket is open and legs spread, as he gazes into the distance. The slight turn of his head from the axis of the body reiterates as well Maybury's easy, relaxed posture. Behind him, carved in white marble relief, is a portrayal of an idealized family group attired in classical drapery. The entire ensemble of pedestal, bronze figure, and relief is framed by a twelve-foot-high, freestanding wall capped by an elaborately carved cornice and supported by a low platform that projects forward.

The Maybury monument shares space in Grand Circus Park with the memorial to Hazen S. Pingree (A-6), Maybury's contemporary and political rival, who also served as mayor of Detroit.

A-8
Russell A. Alger
Memorial Fountain
Daniel Chester French (1850–1931)
and Henry Bacon (1866–1924)
Grand Circus Park, Eastern Half, Woodward Avenue and East Adams Street
1919–1921
Bronze and granite

General Russell A. Alger (1836–1907) served as U.S. senator, governor of Michigan, and secretary of war (under President McKinley). After Alger's death, a memorial society commissioned sculptor Daniel Chester French and architect Henry Bacon to design the Alger Memorial Fountain. Their best-known collaboration is the Lincoln Memorial in Washington, D.C. (1922). French, along with Augustus Saint-Gaudens, was the principal American exponent of the turn-of-the-century Beaux-Arts style, a rich and opulent approach that, in the creation of monuments, emphasized the integration of figure and pedestal as well as statue and site.

In the Alger memorial, a spirited, graceful, and over-life-size personification of the State of Michigan raises her right arm in greeting, while displaying in her left hand a sword and shield decorated with the state's coat of arms. The drapery fluttering from her right shoulder contrasts with the circular shield, a shape that is repeated in the cylindrical pedestal and its round bronze-relief portrait of Alger wreathed in laurel.

The 1997 restoration of the basin, plaza, and park encircling the sculpture has returned this ensemble very close to the harmonious integration it originally enjoyed with its site. The memorial, however, shares its location with a more recent manifestation of civic art, the 1999 *Millennium Bell* (A-9), situated on the western edge of the park. Its silvery finish and vaulting, asymmetric arches offset the traditional forms of Bacon's circular design and the golden-brown patina of French's figure.

A-9
Millennium Bell
Matthew Blake (b. 1965)
and Christopher Turner (b. 1965)
Grand Circus Park, Eastern Half,
Woodward Avenue and East
Adams Street
1999
Stainless steel, painted steel,
and bronze

This work, erected in Grand Circus Park, was commissioned by the city to ring in the new millennium. Matthew Blake and Christopher Turner's proposal was selected after a review of submissions to a competition chaired by Detroit's cultural affairs director at the time, Marilyn L. Wheaton. Detroiters Blake and Turner, who live and make their art in the metropolitan area, had barely six months in which to execute their winning design. Early on they determined to create a new bell for a new age, in effect an industrial bell for an industrial city.

Bells are often housed in towers or belfries, cast in bronze, and emit peals of mellifluous sounds. Instead of following such guidelines, the artists began by choosing a staple manufacturing commodity, steel, as their medium. Turner originated the idea to fold two circular disks of the metal into a triangle, while Blake conceived the soaring, graceful arches that stretch forty feet across the bell and twenty-six feet above it. The height of the bell itself is twenty feet. While evoking Detroit's manufacturing history, the shiny, futuristic bell also resembles a down-turned flower or blossom complete with petals and a pair of stamens or pistils hanging from an arbor.

When the bell is sounded, the bronze clapper strikes the stamen-pistils, or "chimes" (they are actually two mottled-green oxygen tanks), which produce two tones amplified by the outer shell. "Some people asked us about tuning it," Blake observed, "but we were just looking for a sound rather than a note." Since the sculpture's dedication on December 31, 1999, the sounding of the bell has become a New Year's Eve tradition in Detroit.

The original maquette for the bell is in the collection of the Detroit Historical Museums and Society.

A-10
Whale Tower
Wyland (b. 1956)
David Broderick Tower, Woodward Avenue and Witherell Street
1997
Wall painting

A former Detroiter, Robert Wyland (he is known by his surname) attended the College for Creative Studies and now lives in California. There, he painted the first of his series of "whaling walls," inspired by the majestic sight of migrating whales he observed off the coast. The despoiling of waterways around the world caused by over-fishing and pollution would seem to explain the homonymic relationship of the series to the Wailing Wall of Jerusalem. Wyland's goal is to call attention to the beauty and endangered future of creatures of the deep by completing one hundred paintings worldwide by 2008. Highlighting oceanic life in the world's oceans, lakes, rivers, and streams, Wyland's marine murals elicit not only visual pleasure but also environmental awareness on a global scale.

Covering a sixteen-story expanse of one wall of an otherwise unremarkable skyscraper in downtown Detroit, the striking one-hundred-eighty-foot-by-sixty-five-foot *Whale Tower* immediately draws one visually into its blue-green, oceanic depths. The unexpected encounter of Wyland's teeming marine spectacles is all the more appreciated for their anomalous context on urban walls from the landlocked Midwest to New Zealand. Wyland, who donates his time and materials to create his vast, spray-painted seascapes, enlists local volunteers to assist with each project. Detroit's *Whale Tower* is his seventy-sixth such undertaking. For his hometown, the artist represented a natal event: the female of a life-size family of humpback whales guides a newborn calf toward the water's surface while the exuberant male bursts forth above the waves. Below, an escort whale glides along just above an octopus at the far right, which the artist, in a gesture to Detroit, included for its role as the unofficial mascot of the city's hockey team, the Red Wings.

Alas, *Whale Tower* is on occasion temporarily covered by advertisements whose revenue is used to maintain the building on which it is painted.

A-11
The Entrance
John Piet (b. 1946)
Harmonie Park, Randolph Street
and Gratiot Avenue
1975
Painted steel

The City of Detroit Department of Recreation commissioned *The Entrance* as a salute to the International Theatre Olympiad held in Detroit in June 1975. During that event, five hundred amateur performers from forty countries visited the city to participate in numerous theatrical performances. A native Detroiter and graduate of Wayne State University, John Piet received the key to the city during a public ceremony to dedicate his nearly twenty-two-foot sculpture. Although abstract in appearance, the piece can be viewed as a composite of a traditional base and "figure." The figure, inspired by music and dance, rises gracefully to the fan-like appendages spiraling forcefully into space at the top. Moved in 1997 from its former location in Grand Circus Park to a newly designed sunken plaza lined with trees, and raised on a low, concrete pedestal, Piet's red-hued sculpture appears even more graceful and animated in its intimate Harmonie Park setting. Other works by Piet can be seen in Chene and Pingree parks (see C-1, C-20) and in front of the Comerica Building at Fort Street and Washington Boulevard.

A-12
Hard Edge Soft Edge
Hanna Stiebel (1927–2005)
Harmonie Park, Randolph
and Centre Streets
1973
Aluminum and concrete

Nestled in a corner of one of Detroit's numerous small downtown parks, Hanna Stiebel's modestly scaled sculpture is surrounded by trees and backed by a fieldstone wall. Purchased by New Detroit, Inc., and presented to the city, it was installed in the recently redeveloped Harmonie Park in 1973. The subsequent relocation of the sculpture to its present site in the park in 1977 was approved and supervised by Stiebel. Standing in this downtown oasis, the sculpture reflects the artist's sense of the extremes inherent in urban living: soft and hard, permanent and transient, beautiful and tough, noisy and silent. Israeli-born Stiebel, who studied at the College for Creative Studies, is also represented in the Renaissance Center and Blue Cross Blue Shield collections, and by *Rhythms and Vibrations* (1981), a large aluminum sculpture at Meadowbrook in Rochester Hills.

A-13
The Hand of God,
Memorial to Frank Murphy
Carl Milles (1875–1955)
Frank Murphy Hall of Justice,
Saint Antoine Street at Gratiot Avenue
1953 (installed 1970)
Bronze and granite

Frank Murphy (1893–1949) was a well-known Detroit politician whose offices included Recorder's Court judge, mayor of Detroit, governor of Michigan, governor-general of the Philippines, U.S. attorney general, and Supreme Court justice—the last two appointments made by President Franklin D. Roosevelt. After Murphy's death, United Automobile Workers leader Walter P. Reuther and Judge Ira W. Jayne chose Milles's 1953 sculpture, the last he designed at Cranbrook (F-14–17), as a suitable memorial for Murphy. The ten-foot figure of a newly created man, his arms and fingers outspread and head thrown back in amazement at the new world around him, stands lightly on the thumb and forefinger of a mammoth hand dramatically cantilevered from the top of a twenty-six-foot-tall, polished granite shaft. The green patina of the figure silhouetted against the sky and juxtaposed with the slim, black granite pedestal does indeed seem to "lift man up to view the world," as Milles envisioned. Paid for by contributions from the UAW membership, the piece was installed at its present site in 1970. Plans for a reflecting pool to soften the transition from pavement to sculpture were abandoned because of the expense.

A-14
Dancing Hands
Robert Sestok (b. 1946)
Blue Cross Blue Shield of Michigan,
East Lafayette Boulevard at Beaubien Street, Plaza
1999
Painted steel

Urban Stele
Sergio De Giusti (b. 1941)
Blue Cross Blue Shield of Michigan,
East Lafayette Boulevard at Beaubien Street, Plaza
1998–1999
Bronze

Two tall, dark-hued sculptures accentuate the expansive plaza of the headquarters of Blue Cross Blue Shield of Michigan. Commissioned by the health insurance organization, long known for its support of art in public places, *Dancing Hands* by Robert Sestok and *Urban Stele* by Sergio De Giusti each stand nine feet high. The sculptures' dark tones stand out decisively against the varicolored brick façade and plaza of the architectural setting.

The filigreed, painted-steel cylinder by Sestok, with a generous diameter of four-and-one-half feet, fulfills the artist's declared intention: "If you stand and look at it, you see an outline of the images. If you walk around it, the appearance of the piece will change 360 times." Sestok's imagery—dozens of hands, eyes, gabled houses, diminutive human figures, birds, animals, S-curves, and crosses inscribed within circles—alludes to the mission of the insurance agency to help its clients achieve a health-

ful, fulfilling life. *Dancing Hands'* circular shape and array of linked images suggest not only a collective dance of friendship but also the salubrious benefits of community.

Detroiter Sestok studied at the College for Creative Studies and early on became allied with the Cass Corridor artists, a loosely affiliated group known for their improvisatory assemblages; many of them worked out of studios along Cass Avenue near Wayne State University in the 1970s. Sestok also created a welded bronze memorial for the Academy of the Sacred Heart (see F-13).

The stele, a traditional upright form that honors a person or event, has been transformed by Sergio De Giusti to make a contemporary statement.

"The whole piece is like an Italian opera," De Giusti has remarked about *Urban Stele*. "You pull open the curtain and the story unfolds." Standing nine feet tall, this solid, curved bronze slab does indeed offer both a convex "front" and concave "back," or "onstage" and "behind-the-scenes" viewing experiences. The front side displays a vertical sea of faces in both shallow and high relief, the visages becoming more clearly defined toward the top. The artist took care to portray people of different ages, genders, and ethnic backgrounds. On the reverse he represented evolution, from fossilized animals and skeletal remains to symbols and objects, such as pottery and a Navaho blanket, linked to Native American cultures.

Venetian-born De Giusti emigrated to the United States at thirteen; he has exhibited widely in Europe and America. *Transcending*, a collaborative endeavor by De Giusti and David Barr (see A-22), and a relief portrait of General Anthony Wayne (see B-23) are other examples of his expertise in relief sculpture.

Appropriately, given the nature of the commissioning organization and the site, these two works address age-old themes of human history and the desire for wholeness and connections between people. Aesthetically, the pairing of *Dancing Hands* and *Urban Stele* also establishes a dialogue between figurative and abstract visual modes, each enhancing the unique, individual sensibility of the other.

A-15
The Procession (A Family)
John Nick Pappas (b. 1934)
Blue Cross Blue Shield of Michigan, 600 East Lafayette Boulevard,
South Courtyard
1977
Bronze

The Procession (A Family) by John Nick Pappas (partial view shown here) is one of the largest bronze statuary ensembles in the United States. Set in the sprawling, sunken courtyard of the Blue Cross Blue Shield building, the thirteen bronze figures, ten feet in height, are deployed in three separate groupings punctuated by fourteen-foot-tall bronze monoliths and a freestanding fieldstone wall. Stretched out to a length of approximately sixty feet, the procession of figures, who represent the family of man, is intended, according to the artist, to signify "different aspects of human existence: joy, tragedy, and compassion." This broad range of emotions is reinforced visually by figures that not only stand upright but also appear upended and suspended by the vicissitudes of life.

The ensemble's nudity and placement in a reflecting pool, with water's connotation as an essential source of life, attests as well to the primordial, archetypal nature of the figures, who represent emotions or states of being rather than specific individuals. Indeed, as the artist says, they are "a community in microcosm." The over-life-size scale of these personages and their dark patinas were deliberately chosen by Pappas so that they would hold their own against the twenty-two-story Blue Cross Blue Shield tower looming over them. Commissioned in 1973 and completed in 1977, this massive project and technical tour de force (the figures are internally braced to withstand the gusty winds that blow across the court) involved numerous assistants and engineers who worked with the sculptor. Detroit-born Pappas, who taught sculpture at Eastern Michigan University (EMU) for many years, studied at Wayne State University before joining EMU's art faculty.

A 2003 multifigural ensemble by Pappas, a depiction of early settlers of Wyandotte, Michigan, is located at BASF Park in the city (see D-17).

A-16
Victory and Progress
John Massey Rhind (1860–1936)
Wayne County Building, Cadillac Square and Randolph Street
1898–1902
Sheet bronze

To flank the soaring central tower of the majestic Beaux-Arts Wayne County Building, designed by John and Arthur Scott and Company, New York, sculptor John Massey Rhind created two allegorical groups representing Victory and Progress. Each of these animated ensembles consists of a draped female figure standing in a classical chariot drawn by three rearing horses. Each team of horses is led by two partially clad, youthful males. Made of sheet bronze joined in sections, and now weathered to a rich green patina, the two groups stand out vividly against the sky and are a colorful crown for this sumptuous limestone and sandstone building. Four smaller female figures representing Law, Commerce, Agriculture, and Mechanics ornament the corners of the tower above. Born in Scotland, Rhind studied in Paris and in 1898 settled in New York, where he became well-known for his numerous decorations for federal and municipal buildings. Detroiter Edward Wagner (1855–1922) was responsible for the building's carved ornamentation, including the cherubs and wreaths above windows and the pediment, showing General Anthony Wayne and Native Americans concluding a treaty.

A-17
Christopher Columbus
Augusto Rivalta (1837–1925)
East Jefferson Avenue and Randolph Street
1910
Bronze and travertine

An initiative to honor Columbus (1451–1506), Italy's most famous son, on the four hundredth anniversary of his death was begun by Vincenzo Giuliano, the editor of Detroit's *Italian Tribune of America*. Italian sculptor Augusto Rivalta, who contributed a sculptural group to the *Victor Emmanuel II* monument in Rome (1888–1892), was so enthused over the commission that he waived payment for his labors. The larger-than-life bust, mounted on a tall pedestal, portrays the explorer as a visionary, his head raised high and his gaze fixed on the distance. The powerful thrust of the shoulders, placed on a diagonal to the head and pedestal, reinforces the strong impact of this image of the early explorer. The complexity of the pedestal, with its heavy foliate cornice, its bronze plaque, and the suggestion of the prow and stern of a boat at the base, adds a distinctive note to the piece. Once located at the north end of Washington Boulevard, at Grand Circus Park, the sculpture and base were cleaned, restored, and moved to the present location in 1988.

A-18
George Washington
Donald DeLue (1897–1988)
East Jefferson Avenue
and Randolph Street
1959
Bronze and granite

Presented to the city of Detroit in 1966 by the Masons of Michigan "in commemoration of ten centuries of Freemasonry (966–1966)," according to the inscription on the pedestal, Donald DeLue's statue of George Washington (1732–1799) depicts "the father of our country" displaying the regalia of Masonry. In this larger-than-life portrayal, Washington holds a gavel and wears a fringed "apron" and pendant decorated with Masonic emblems. The Masons, a social and fraternal organization with worldwide membership, has numbered among its illustrious members not only the first president but also Benjamin Franklin, Mozart, and Voltaire.

Sculptor DeLue, who maintained a studio in New Jersey, was trained at the School of the Museum of Fine Arts, Boston, and specialized in bronzes of historical figures such as Washington, Franklin, and Jefferson. His depiction of Washington is stolidly frontal and reserved, as the president gazes resolutely ahead, attired, except for the Masonry accessories, in the clothing of an everyday citizen of his era.

A-19
Pylon
Isamu Noguchi (1904–1988)
Philip A. Hart Civic Center Plaza,
Jefferson and Woodward Avenues
1973
Stainless steel

The pylon, 120 feet high and seven feet square, was designed as a dramatic terminus for Detroit's main street, Woodward Avenue. Reminiscent of such age-old forms as obelisk, tower, or beacon, *Pylon* also marks the city's waterfront and its other axis of transportation, the busy Detroit River waterway. In this monumental work, composed of meticulously joined steel sections, Isamu Noguchi exhibited his preference for simple forms and his attention to detail. Rising from a low rectangular plinth, the pylon subtly makes a quarter turn as it soars to its full height, directing the viewer toward the fountain to the right, also designed by Noguchi (A-20). In Noguchi's overall design for the plaza, the sleek, flawless finish of both pylon and fountain creates bright, reflective surfaces and clean geometric shapes. These harmonize with the massive glass and steel cylindrical towers of the 1977 Renaissance Center (by architect John Portman), now General Motors World Headquarters, which rise commandingly at the eastern end of the plaza.

A-20
Horace E. Dodge and Son Memorial Fountain
Isamu Noguchi (1904–1988)
Philip A. Hart Civic Center Plaza, Jefferson and Woodward Avenues
1973 (erected 1978)
Stainless steel

Answering an appeal from Mayor Jerome Cavanaugh and *Detroit News* editor Martin Hayden, Anna Thomson Dodge, the widow of automobile magnate Horace E. Dodge, bequeathed two million dollars to erect a fountain as a memorial to her husband and son, Horace Dodge Jr. Los Angeles–born sculptor Isamu Noguchi was selected to do the fountain and eventually designed the plaza and pylon (A-19) as well. The thirty-foot-high fountain, which forms the focus of the plaza, is composed of a stainless steel ring suspended daringly between two inwardly canted supports. Columnar jets of water from the basin below can interact in a variety of ways with the downward sprays from the ring above. It is set into a broad plaza of over ten acres, with the Detroit River and the skyline of Windsor, Ontario, beyond serving as one backdrop and the higher, more dramatic skyline of Detroit as the other. The shallow, bowl-like depression surrounding the fountain encourages the spectator to walk into and participate in the water display. The fountain's sophisticated engineering and simple but elegant form, its powerful jets of water, and its dramatic setting combine to create an almost futuristic environment. As Noguchi said, "I wanted to make a new fountain, a fountain which represents our times and our relationship to outer space."

**International Memorial
to the Underground
Railroad**
Ed Dwight (b. 1933)
The Gateway to Freedom
Philip A Hart Civic Center
Plaza, Jefferson and Wood-
ward Avenues, Detroit
2001
Bronze and granite

Tower of Freedom
Civic Esplanade
Riverside Drive East,
between McDougall Avenue
and Goyeau Street, Windsor,
Ontario
2001
Bronze and granite

The Underground Railroad, neither underground nor a railway, was a clandestine network of routes and shelters that allowed enslaved African Americans to travel northward to freedom. White and black abolitionists alike hid and conducted thousands of liberty seekers to safety. Detroit was one of the next-to-the-last stops on the journey; across the Detroit River, in Windsor, Canada, slavery was prohibited. Both cities are the sites of complementary monuments dedicated in 2001 to the Underground Railroad. Underwritten by Detroit 300, the International Underground Railroad Monument Collaborative of Detroit, and the Underground Railroad Monument Committee of Windsor, the two large-scale ensembles were commissioned in honor of Detroit's 2001 tercentenary.

Sculptor Ed Dwight won the competition for the commission with his design: companion figural groups portraying the successful arrival at these desperately sought destinations—Detroit and Windsor—after an arduous, perilous, and long trek north. Located adjacent to the Detroit River, Detroit's twelve-foot-tall *Gateway to Freedom* represents eight figures in a pyramidal cluster hovering at the very edge of the bank; six follow the gaze and urging of their "conductor," Detroit shipowner George DeBaptiste, to take in the view of their goal: Windsor. Behind them, a young boy and girl turn backward toward Detroit, as the boy beckons others to follow.

Windsor's *Tower of Freedom* is located about two city blocks inland. Here, the refugees face Canada, as a Quaker woman at the right welcomes them to a new life. A towering, twenty-two-foot-high granite shaft echoes the jubilant, upraised arms of the central male protagonist. At its summit, a stylized bronze flame "burns" eternally. As in the Detroit piece, a youth stands behind the primary group: a bewildered young girl holding a doll turns to look at the river she has just traversed.

Aesthetically, the linking of gazes from one side of the river to the other demonstrates Dwight's solution to the challenge of relating two figural groups separated by a broad, half-mile-wide waterway. He also captured the often-contradictory feelings of people facing new circumstances with an admixture of anticipation and concern, no matter how abhorrent the situation from which they have escaped. As Dwight explained, "I want people to say, 'My God, I can feel what this was like.'"

The Denver-based artist, who served as a pilot in the U.S. Air Force and trained as an astronaut in the space program, turned to art after his retirement from the service, becoming, in his "second" career of some twenty-five years, a prolific realist sculptor. His two-part ensemble represents the first international testimonial not only to nineteenth-century freedom seekers but also to the "engineers," "conductors," and generous hosts on both sides of the border who risked their lives to liberate victims of slavery.

A-22
Transcending
David Barr (b. 1939) and Sergio De Giusti (b. 1941)
West Jefferson Avenue at Woodward Avenue
2001–2003
Steel, bronze, and granite

Transcending, whose most visible element is a six-story-high arch, was a gift to the people of Detroit on the occasion of the tercentenary of the city's founding in 1701. Its construction was spearheaded by the Michigan Labor Legacy Project as a tribute to the history, principles, and spirit of the labor movement. David Barr, one of *Transcending*'s two creators, described the piece as "an experience more than just a symbol. You have to get inside of it, stand beneath the arches, walk along the path, read the quotations. It's not one element, but all taken together."

WE WANT MORE SCHOOLHOUSES AND LESS JAILS

Indeed, arrayed in a spiral beneath a gleaming steel arch, whose faceted inner rims resemble a gear, are fourteen dark-green polished-granite boulders that have been split in half. Affixed to each is a bronze relief—the work of Sergio De Giusti—detailing various struggles and achievements in the history of American labor. The boulders' human scale (they range in height from four to six feet) offers the direct, one-to-one engagement that draws the onlooker from one plaque to the next, creating a narrative delineating the struggles and achievements of laboring men and women. Placed like way stations along a spiral path laid out on a circular dais seventy-five feet in diameter, the boulders and their plaques offer a human counterpoint to the arch soaring above. *Transcending* also features a round "Voices of Labor" plinth, on which are inscribed blunt and feisty quotations from labor activists: "Don't mourn, organize," orders Joe Hill. "Women were in labor before men were born," Myra Wolfgang wittily asserts. "The people united will never be defeated," declares Cesar Chavez.

The "arch," as many describe it, is actually a circle, as sculptor Barr has maintained, since its curving form seems to emerge from or descend into the ground rather than rest on its surface. Notably, it is incomplete at its apex, implying that the evolution of the labor movement is ongoing and open to future developments. At night the gap is bridged by an intense beam of light, which suggests the hope that unity is within reach.

Sculptors and collaborators Barr and De Giusti share a number of experiences: they both grew up in Detroit, studied art at Wayne State University, and continue to live and work in the metropolitan area. Nonetheless, their artworks exemplify contrary sensibilities: Barr's is essentially abstract, whereas De Giusti's is primarily representational. Here, in their first joint endeavor, their divergent aesthetics melded, like the many voices of the labor movement, into a whole greater than the sum of its parts.

For other works by Barr, see E-1 and E-2; for De Giusti, see A-14 and B-23.

A-23
Memorial to Joe Louis
Robert Graham (b. 1938)
Woodward and Jefferson Avenues
1986
Bronze and painted steel

Mexican-born Robert Graham has long been known for his formal, classical sculptures of the human figure. Now a U.S. citizen and long-term resident of California, Graham was commissioned by *Sports Illustrated* magazine to create a memorial to boxing champion Joe Louis (1914–1981). His conception concentrates on the legendary physical strength of Louis, who grew up in Detroit and was world heavyweight boxing champion from 1937 to 1949. Rather than modeling the entire figure of Louis, Graham focused, like many twentieth-century sculptors before him, on a characteristic feature, namely the tensed arm and clenched fist of the pugilist. The twenty-eight-foot-long arm modeled to scale (one inch equals one foot) embodies the determined will and fighting spirit of the boxer and, by extension, of Detroit and the nation he represented. Though the sculpture is frequently referred to locally as "The Fist," it actually consists of Louis's hand and arm suspended from a four-legged steel armature. A larger-than-life, full-length bronze of Louis in fighting gear—shoes, boxing shorts, and gloves—by Edward N. Hamilton may be seen in the main lobby of nearby Cobo Center.

The memorial's location, at the busy intersection of Detroit's two main thoroughfares, with its visual cacophony of light poles, traffic signals, and street signs, does not perhaps show the sculpture to its best advantage.

A-24
The Spirit of Detroit
Marshall Fredericks (1908–1998)
Coleman A. Young Municipal Center, Woodward and Jefferson Avenues
1955–1958
Bronze, gilt, and marble

The Spirit of Detroit is the city's best-known outdoor sculpture. The architects of the renamed City-County Building, Harley, Ellington, and Day (now Harley, Ellington, Pierce, Yee Associates), planned the Woodward Avenue façade as a backdrop for this dramatic sixteen-foot-high sculpture, with its green patina. Created by Detroit-area sculptor Marshall Fredericks (see also A-27, C-12, D-19, F-3, F-21), who studied with Carl Milles and later taught at the Cranbrook Academy of Art, *The Spirit of Detroit* was commissioned in 1955 and dedicated in 1958. Stretching twenty-three feet fingertip to fingertip, the huge seated figure, representing the spirit of humanity, holds in his left hand a gilt-bronze sphere (with emanating rays) symbolizing God, and in his right hand a family group embodying all human relationships, also in gilt bronze. Thus, God, as an inscription on a plaque in front of the sculpture reveals, "through the spirit of man is manifested in the family, the noblest human relationship." Serving as a backdrop is the thirty-six-by-forty-five-foot semicircular "Symbol Wall," bearing raised reliefs of the seals of the city and county, along with the incised passage "Now the Lord is that Spirit: and where the Spirit of the Lord is, there is liberty" (2 Cor. 3:17).

The erection of a fence and planting of a flower bed in front of the figure runs counter to Fredericks's preference for an open, unadorned space between statue and spectator.

A-25
Passo di danza (Dance Step)
Giacomo Manzu (1908–1991)
One Woodward Plaza Building,
Jefferson and Woodward Avenues
1963
Bronze

In 1961 Giacomo Manzu visited the United States, where he met Detroit architect Minoru Yamasaki (1912–1986), who commissioned the Italian artist to complete sculptures for two of his buildings in Detroit. (The other, *Nymph and Faun*, is in the courtyard of Wayne State University's McGregor Memorial Conference Center; see B-25). Born in Bergamo, Italy, where he first studied, Manzu subsequently attended the academy in Verona before settling in Milan in 1930 where he received his first sculpture commissions.

Modeled after his wife, the eleven-foot bronze was the first of Manzu's works to be publicly displayed in the United States. To complement the elegance of Yamasaki's building, originally the Michigan Consolidated Gas Building, Manzu depicted a graceful nude dancer on toe, her hands lifted over her head to uncoil her hair, which further elongates her lithe silhouette. She is placed on a lozenge-shaped, tapered base that functions as a fountain. The small, rectangular reflecting pool, originally much larger, is bordered by low shrubs.

A-26
Gomidas
Arto Tchakmakchian (b. 1933)
West Jefferson and Woodward Avenues
1980–1981
Bronze and granite

This sculpture of Father Gomidas Vartabed (1869–1935) was erected in memory of the 1,500,000 Armenians who perished during the 1915–1923 genocide perpetrated by the government of Turkey. Detroit Armenians raised the funds to commission and install, on land donated by the city, the ten-and-a-half-foot-tall Gomidas on a granite pedestal. Designed by Canadian sculptor Arto Tchakmakchian, this image of the sad, mournful cleric stands enveloped in a coarse, heavy, full-length robe. The stoic curate raises his head and chin slightly, as if looking beyond the horror he experienced.

A composer and musicologist, Gomidas was imprisoned with 300 fellow Armenians apprehended on April 24, 1915; eventually released through diplomatic efforts, Gomidas later died, broken in spirit, in exile in Paris. A sense of the pain he endured is conveyed by his stance, in which one arm, bent in a ninety-degree angle across his chest, clutches the arm at his side, as if attempting to restrain the grief inside. In contrast to the rigid, angular placement of his arms, broad, thick folds of cloth flow and curve along the length of his slender physique. The dark, black patina of the bronze serves as well to deepen the sense of the tragedy of Gomidas, the Armenian people, and all who suffer and perish in such atrocities.

A-27
Victory Eagle and Pylons
Marshall Fredericks (1908–1998)
UAW-Ford National Programs Center,
151 West Jefferson Avenue
1950
Marble

The earliest sketches for the façade of the UAW-Ford Center (formerly the Veterans Memorial Building) by architects Harley, Ellington, and Day (now Harley, Ellington, Pierce, Yee Associates) include this work by sculptor Marshall Fredericks, which explains in part the successful integration of the sculpture and building. The thirty-foot marble eagle clutching the laurel and palm, symbols of glory and victory, in its talons projects in high relief from an expansive wall of the same material. The bird's boldly stylized V-shape catches light and throws dramatic shadows across the marble façade. Each of the six marble pylons arranged along the walkway to the west (they were originally aligned along the east walkway) depicts an event in the military history of Detroit or the United States: the explorer Cadillac—improbably accompanied by Father Gabriel Richard (C-9), who lived much later—at the founding of Detroit; Chief Pontiac signing the peace treaty ending the Indian War; Admiral Perry and the Battle of Lake Erie during the War of 1812; President Lincoln and General Grant; Theodore Roosevelt and Commodore Perry in Spanish-American War scenes; and a symbolic female figure with the World War I slogan "To Make the World Safe for Democracy." The seventh pylon refers to the end of World War II, with incised hand, branch, stars, and patriotic inscriptions.

The design was thus conceived on two scales, namely, an eagle meant to be visible from a distance and incised pylons intended for close viewing. A similar principle obtains in the nearby *Transcending* monument as well (A-22).

A 1997 renovation of the building opened a large window high on the façade, which compromises the simplicity of the original design.

A-28
Abraham Lincoln
Gutzon Borglum (1867–1941)
UAW-Ford National Programs Center,
151 West Jefferson Avenue
1918
Marble and granite

Best known for his colossal portrait heads of presidents Washington, Jefferson, Lincoln, and Theodore Roosevelt carved on Mount Rushmore in South Dakota (1927–1941), Gutzon Borglum, the son of Danish pioneers, attended schools in his home state of Kansas before studying in Paris in the 1890s, where he was most influenced by French sculptor Auguste Rodin (see B-6). Borglum settled in New York City in 1902 and produced in 1908 the six-ton marble head of Lincoln for the Library of Congress, which was followed, ten years later, by this smaller version. The sculpture reveals Borglum's ability to transform marble into lifelike surfaces. The monumental head seems to be emerging from an unfinished block of marble, suggesting the figure's upper torso. The slight turn of the head to the left, the faraway gaze of the downcast eyes, and the furrowed brow convey the oppressive burdens and sadness carried by this most compassionate of presidents. The work was given to the Detroit Institute of Arts by Ralph H. Booth in 1924. It was reinstalled in 1958 on a base designed by Marshall Fredericks (see A-24) after years in storage at the museum. Badly vandalized at one point, the present nose is a restoration.

After being displayed for many years on the north lawn of the art institute, the sculpture was relocated to its present site in downtown Detroit, courtesy of the museum. It has been placed in an intimate, sunken court dedicated to Civil War veterans of Michigan.

A-29
Untitled
W. Robert Youngman (b. 1927)
Comerica Building, 411 West Lafayette Boulevard
1970
Concrete

One of the important design features of the Comerica Building is
its union of art and architecture. Working from the beginning of
the project with Detroit architect Louis G. Redstone, Illinois-born
W. Robert Youngman designed twenty-six cast concrete relief panels nineteen feet tall that wrap around three sides of the building.
(Two are visible in the accompanying photograph.) In these panels,
Youngman chose to celebrate Detroit's worldwide fame for automotive design and production. The sculptor employed machine
shapes (cogs, gears, discs, dies), which he arranged in varied clusters
so that no panel repeats another. Thus, from one section to the next,
the sculptor created an image of continual industrial activity. The
execution of the panels was a technological feat in itself. Working in
a northwest Detroit warehouse, Youngman welded together metal
pieces that were then pressed into sheets of Styrofoam. These sheets
became the molds from which he made his cast concrete reliefs. As
set into place, the panels, with their rough and irregular patterns
and sandblasted surfaces, provide a handsome contrast to the austere black granite and steel building. Other cast concrete work by
Youngman is located in the lobby of the Webber Memorial Building
of Grace Hospital, Detroit, and on the exterior of the Michael Berry
International Terminal at Detroit Metropolitan Airport.

General Thaddeus Kosciuszko
Leonard Marconi (1836–1899)
Michigan Avenue and Third Street
1978
Bronze and granite

Often referred to as the "hero of two worlds," General Thaddeus Kosciuszko (1746–1817), like his contemporary, General Casimir Pulaski (see D-16), fought not only for the freedom of his native Poland but also for the United States during the Revolutionary War. An expert military engineer, he oversaw the construction of fortifications, including West Point, New York, shortly after his arrival in 1776, and later took part in the siege of Charleston, South Carolina. Rewarded by Congress with the rank of brigadier general, Kosciuszko returned to Poland in 1784 to direct the continuing efforts of the Poles to resist Russian domination.

Kosciuszko's heroic-size equestrian monument (twelve feet tall), positioned on an elevated pedestal (ten feet high) above Michigan Avenue, is superbly sited a short distance from Detroit's downtown area. From his lofty vantage point, the general, astride his horse, doffs his hat, seeming to extend a hearty welcome to all who approach the city's center. The passionate freedom fighter is presented less as a military officer and more as a humanitarian citizen of the world. The original of Detroit's *Kosciuszko* was modeled by the Polish Italian Leonard Marconi in 1889 and stands on the grounds of Wawel Castle in Kraków, Poland. Born in Warsaw, Marconi was a member of a family of architect-sculptors prominent in the nineteenth century. This cast was a gift to the City of Detroit from the people of Kraków in honor of the American bicentennial of 1976.

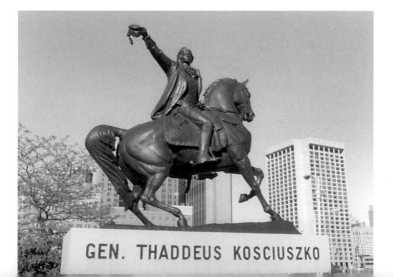

GEN. THADDEUS KOSCIUSZKO

A-31
Kevin C. Flaherty Memorial
Hubert Massey (b. 1958)
Internal Revenue Service, Detroit Computing Center,
Michigan Avenue and Third Street
1995
Granite and concrete

This large, inclined disc, set behind a curved, waist-high "wall" that faces Michigan Avenue, depicts in considerable detail the history of Detroit as interpreted by artist Hubert Massey. Born in Flint, Detroiter Massey painted billboards for many years and has created a number of muralistic compositions in different media, including examples at Detroit's Atheneum Hotel and the Charles H. Wright Museum of African American History. The twelve-foot-diameter disc was commissioned as the centerpiece for this memorial to Kevin C. Flaherty (1958–1994), a leader in the development of the IRS facility.

Employing a tondo, a circular format once used by Renaissance painters, Massey divided his striking black-and-white composition

into quadrants to narrate the significant events of Detroit's history. The story opens with a scene of Native Americans amid their villages that is dramatically contrasted in quadrant two with the migration of workers at the turn of the century to a skyscraper-studded metropolis. Straddling the second and third sections is a trio of singers gathered around a microphone who represent the emergence of the sounds of Motown. Within quadrant three, the rebirth of Detroit is symbolized by images of the Renaissance Center and People Mover (see A-36a–g). In the last segment, the future of the city is embodied in the personas of a student-architect and a worker wearing a hard hat.

Massey's skillful manipulation of scale, variation of the thickness and thinness of contours, and interweaving of multiple episodes and scenes enable him to tell his story swiftly and boldly. Like an ancient petrograph (a carving incised into rock), the white lines and areas of Massey's pictorial history were actually achieved by abrading the veneer of black graphite to expose the white surface underneath.

The low-rise wall that screens the circular, ground-hugging memorial, along with built-in benches and planters, forms both a physical and psychic buffer from the heavily trafficked intersection. Within this semi-sheltered precinct the visitor can review the ongoing history of Detroit while remembering honoree Flaherty as an exemplar of a conscientious citizenry essential to the well-being of Detroit and cities everywhere.

The artist's command of large-scale compositions may also be appreciated in his nine-hundred-square-foot central panel for *Patterns of Detroit* (B-12).

A-32
Deliquescence
John Chamberlain (b. 1927)
Patrick V. McNamara Federal Building,
477 Michigan Avenue at Cass Avenue, Plaza
1979–1981
Painted steel and chromium-plated steel

Deliquescence, with its red, white, and blue patina and structure of salvaged automobile parts, seems a particularly relevant sculpture for the plaza of a U.S. government building located in the Motor City. Since the late 1950s, Indiana-born John Chamberlain has been fabricating abstract sculptures out of discarded vehicles. He cuts, twists, bends, and welds bumpers, fenders, doors, and hoods into either freestanding objects or wall-mounted reliefs. *Deliquescence* was in fact constructed in Florida, where the sculptor now lives, from parts found in a local junkyard. Commissioned by the Art in Architecture Program of the United States General Services Administration in 1979, *Deliquescence* was completed in 1981 and transported to Detroit in 1982.

The sixteen-foot-tall sculpture is set into a shallow, sunken, rectangular area and surrounded by plantings that soften the broad, triangular plaza. Despite its sharp, harsh edges, *Deliquescence*, as the title proclaims, appears to be melting and collapsing, as if indeed approaching its own built-in obsolescence. While such overt commentary might be disclaimed by Chamberlain, his recycling of scrap materials demonstrates the remarkable process of transforming cast-off components into artful new configurations.

Removed from the plaza in 2005 for conservation, *Deliquescence* will be reinstalled in the near future.

A-33
Wish Tree for Detroit
Yoko Ono (b. 1933)
Grand River Avenue and East Park Place
2000
Tree, granite, and bronze

Internationally known performance and installation artist Yoko Ono first proposed to Detroit collectors Lila and Gilbert Silverman in 1998 a *Wish Tree for Detroit*. With the Silvermans' support, *Wish Tree for Detroit* was installed in Detroit's Times Square/Robert L. Hurst Jr. Park in 2000. Ono's "living sculpture" is made up of a ginkgo tree, a granite stone, and a bronze plaque. One of the earliest permanent Wish Tree installations (others are in Brazil, California, Italy, and Japan), this poetic work embodies both spirit ("happiness, peace, and joy" according to the artist) and matter (the quarried granite).

Ono has presented various "wish" installations and performances since the 1990s. One early example from 1991 simply advised visitors to "make a wish when the sun hits." In 1996 she began incorporating actual trees in temporary indoor or outdoor installations, favoring long-lived trees with tenacious roots. Growing up in Japan, she was deeply impressed by the trees in temple gardens, their branches laden with tiny rolls of paper that resemble blossoms. Bearing the writers' hopes and prayers, these bits of paper embody the ceaseless human desire for personal or universal fulfillment. For Detroit, Ono chose a ginkgo, a tree that has been cultivated in Japan for centuries, because of its hardiness.

The bronze plaque mounted on the roughly cut granite instructs the viewer to "Whisper your wish / to the bark of the tree." As the artist reiterated at the piece's dedication, "I believe we can create a more positive future through wishing." The construction of the Rosa Parks Transit Center (2007–2008) on the site has necessitated the temporary removal of *Wish Tree for Detroit*.

A-34
General Alexander Macomb
Adolph Alexander Weinman (1870–1952)
Washington Boulevard at Michigan Avenue
1906–1908
Bronze and granite

Alexander Macomb (1782–1841) was born to a wealthy Detroit family (his father was a partner of John Jacob Astor); the Macombs owned not only most of Macomb County but Grosse Ile and Belle Isle as well. Choosing a military career, Macomb distinguished himself at the battle of Plattsburgh, New York, during the War of 1812. In 1906, Adolph Alexander Weinman was selected in a competition to memorialize this early Michigan hero. Although not well-known, the thirty-six-year-old sculptor had worked with Daniel Chester French, the preeminent American sculptor (see A-8), and Augustus Saint-Gaudens. He portrayed Macomb as a dashing officer whose vitality is suggested by the slightly off-center stance of the figure and furl of the wind-blown cape. A low wall, accented by three bronze cannons, partly encloses a broad, circular terrace on which statue and pedestal are situated. The Macomb memorial was so well received that several years later Weinman was asked to execute the William Cotter Maybury Monument, unveiled in Grand Circus Park in 1912 (A-7).

Another statue of Macomb, by Frank Varga (see B-14), stands in front of the Macomb County Court Building in Mt. Clemens.

A-35
Color Cubes
David Rubello (b. 1935)
Julian C. Madison Building, 1420 Washington Boulevard
at Clifford Street, North Wall
1973
Wall painting

Painter and sculptor David Rubello, who studied abroad (Italy and Germany) and in the Detroit area (College for Creative Studies), made his first geometric paintings in the 1960s. Commissioned to

create a downtown mural in 1972, he designed *Color Cubes* as a tall, narrow image (fifty by twenty-five feet) to fill just the segment of a large wall nearest the sidewalk and street. The resulting painting may be read as a four-story stack of blue, yellow, orange, and burnt red cubic shapes aligned along a central spine or axis. Notably, the interlocking cubes seem to shift and flip (the artist describes them as "flippable forms"), alternately appearing solid and transparent, two-dimensional and three-dimensional, and receding and pushing forward. This continuous, restless interplay of geometry, space, and color conveys something of the flux and dynamic energy that underlies the seeming solidity and secure structure of the world. Although composed of basic elements, *Color Cubes* belies its title and rewards the viewer with a vivacious, shifting display of form and color, no mean feat to achieve on a large expanse of solid brick wall.

A-36a–g
Art in the Stations
Detroit People Mover, Various Locations, Downtown Detroit
1984–1987

From 1984 to 1987, fifteen artists were commissioned to design works of art for the thirteen stations on the three-mile-long monorail that encircles downtown Detroit. The results are as varied and lively as the architecture of the stations is uniformly geometric and functional. This diversity is due in part to the array of materials employed by the artists, including neon light (Stephen Antonakas), baked enamel (Glen Michaels; F-5), two bronzes (J. Seward Johnson and Kirk Newman), an enamel painting on alucobond (Charles McGee), two mosaics (one by Gerome Kamrowski and a collaborative effort by Larry Ebel and Linda Scarlett), and eight ceramic tile pieces (Jun Kaneko, Joyce Kozloff, Alvin Loving Jr., Allie McGhee, Diana Pancioli, Tom Phardel, Farley Tobin, George Woodman). Since then two additional sculptures have been added, one by Marshall Fredericks (see also A-24) and another by Sandra Osip.

A-36a
At the Cadillac Center station, Diana Pancioli (b. 1942) devised a formal scheme of tall, slender arches that recall the arcades and grand spaces of railroad waiting rooms of the past. The rich olive greens of the vintage (c. 1950) Pewabic tiles Pancioli incorporated into her plan are counterpointed by turquoises, purples, blues, and golds. Her design, titled *In Honor of Mary Chase Stratton*, commemorates the founder of Detroit's famed Pewabic Pottery. Pancioli also utilized vintage Pewabic tiles in a wall work for the University Health Center (B-4).

A-36b

In contrast, Jun Kaneko (b. 1942) created a design that seems to be in perpetual motion. Diagonal stripes of pink, yellow, and orange juxtaposed with darker hues move restlessly across the walls of the Broadway station. Head of ceramics at the Cranbrook from 1979 to 1986, the Japanese-born Kaneko now resides in Omaha, Nebraska. A recent wall work by the artist has been added to the Beaumont Hospital Collection (see F-5).

A-36c

On the lower level of the same station, Detroiter Charles McGee (b. 1924) focused on children and animals in *The Blue Nile*. Executed on four panels of alucobond, five children in wildly patterned garb, as well as snakes, birds, centipedes, and a cat and mouse, are interwoven in a lively, animated frieze of kinetic energy.

A-36d
At the Michigan Avenue station, Kirk Newman (b. 1926), a Kalamazoo resident, created fourteen cast bronze silhouettes of rushing commuters in *On the Move,* as he titled his cast of businesspeople, laborers, children, and shoppers. Theatrically outlined against gray tile walls, the hurrying figures dash from ground-level entrance to upper-level platform. The largest of these flattened personages, legs spread wide, spans a twenty-three-foot width and bounds up the escalator in a single leap.

A-36e
Detroit New Morning by Alvin Loving Jr. (1935–2005) at the Millender Center station sparkles with metallic lusters and a joie de vivre in its semi-abstract delineation of rainbow and clouds in combination with calligraphic semicircles, diagonals, and right-angled lines. The soft color graduations—from yellow to pink to blue—of the background are punctuated by Loving's exuberant linear elements, which sometimes extend beyond the confines of the mural's frame. A former Detroiter, Loving lived and worked in New York after the mid-1960s.

A-36f

A resident in Ann Arbor for many years, Gerome Kamrowski (1914–2004), an American exponent of Surrealism, was long fascinated with imaginary hybrid creatures. In a dazzling Venetian glass mosaic of vivid orange hues, a covey of beasts from land, sea, and air sport fantastic heads, bodies, and multiple appendages as they cavort and disport themselves along two fifteen-foot-long walls of the Joe Louis Arena station. As the title *Voyage* suggests, they, along with the People Mover patrons, have embarked on a magical tour or journey. An acrylic on paper maquette for Kamrowski's murals is on view as part of the collection of Detroit Receiving Hospital and University Health Center (see B-4).

A-36g

The bronze relief sculpture *Progression II* by Sandra Osip (b. 1948) was added to the street level of the Fort/Cass station in 1992. Its oversized paired nautilus shells, with their mottled green patina, add a welcome organic presence to the station's cool, utilitarian architecture. A former Detroiter, sculptor Osip now lives and works in New York.

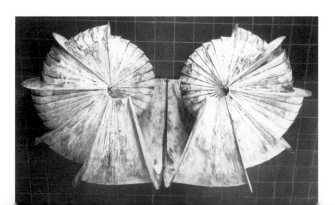

CULTURAL CENTER

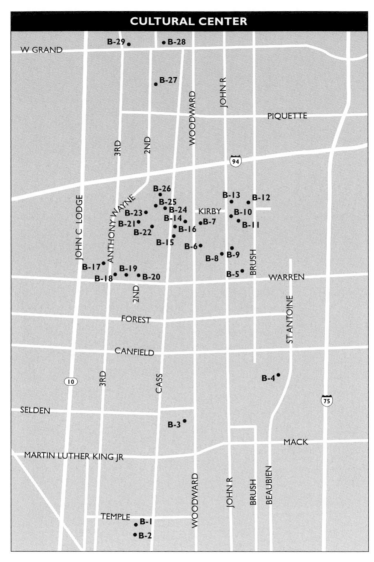

B-1. Robert Burns
B-2. Pink Landscape–Three Trusses Plus
B-3. Trilogy
B-4. Art in Detroit Receiving Hospital and University Health Center
B-5. Sentry
B-6. The Thinker
B-7. Gracehoper
B-8. Jeune fille et sa suite (Young Woman and Her Suitors)
B-9. Curved Form with Rectangle and Space
B-10. Hip and Spine (Stone Chair Setting)
B-11. Normanno Wedge I
B-12. Patterns of Detroit
B-13. Arch: Montrose
B-14. Mikolaj Kopernik (Nicolaus Copernicus)
B-15. The River of Knowledge
B-16. Exploration
B-17. Marquette, LaSalle, Cadillac, and Richard
B-18. Untitled
B-19. Helios Trail
B-20. Continuity
B-21. Automotive Mural
B-22. Wings of Learning
B-23. General Anthony Wayne
B-24. Midmien
B-25. Nymph and Faun
B-26. Nordkyn
B-27. Silverbolt (Detroit Horse Power IV)
B-28. An American Lightbow and Jennifer's Butterfly
B-29. Continuity Tower

B. Cultural Center

B-1
Robert Burns
George A. Lawson (1832–1904)
Cass Park, Second Avenue and Temple Street
1921
Bronze and granite

Robert Burns (1759–1796), Scotland's national poet, wrote some of the most familiar and best-loved poems—"My Love Is Like a Red, Red Rose"—and songs in the English language. His "Auld Lang Syne" and "Comin' Thro' the Rye" are sung around the world. This nine-foot memorial sculpture, marking the formal entrance to Cass Park and erected by Detroit's Burns Club and the Jean Armour Women's Auxiliary, is a cast of a statue of Burns at Ayr, Scotland, by Scottish (b. Edinburgh) artist George A. Lawson. The dedication ceremonies in 1921 included a parade led by Walter Scott, a descendant of the Scottish poet and novelist Sir Walter Scott (1771–1832). A young and handsome Burns, known for his lively verse and spirited life, has been caught here at what seems to be an uncharacteristic moment of quiet and reflection. Inset bronze reliefs on the sides and back of the pedestal illustrate verses from various poems by Burns.

B-2
Pink Landscape—Three Trusses Plus
James L. Lawton (b. 1944)
Cass Park, Second Avenue at Ledyard Street
1978
Painted steel

Pink Landscape—Three Trusses Plus commands a grassy, circular plot near the center of Cass Park. Commissioned by the City of Detroit's Department of Recreation from sculptor James L. Lawton, who teaches at Michigan State University, the trio of parallel tubes seems to emerge from the ground vertically and descend quickly back beneath the earth, like a subterranean pipeline appearing temporarily aboveground. The small, cylindrical components, superimposed at various angles over the larger ones, mitigate the harsh symmetry and spare character of the six-foot-high-by-twenty-foot-long piece. Initially a hot-pink color, the sculpture has been repainted a noticeably paler shade of pink. Serendipitously, the close conjunction of *Pink Landscape* and *Robert Burns* (B-1) in Cass Park highlights the often spirited coexistence of figurative and abstract idioms in public art.

B-3
Trilogy
Louise Nevelson (1899–1988)
Orchestra Place Courtyard,
Woodward Avenue
and Parsons Street
1979
Painted steel and aluminum

Tucked away in a suburban setting since its completion in 1979, Louise Nevelson's *Trilogy* was relocated in 1998 to the Detroit Symphony Orchestra's Orchestra Place courtyard. Originally titled *Bendix Trilogy* when commissioned by the Bendix Corporation for its Southfield offices in 1978, the trio of sculptures was offered to the symphony by Allied Signal Automotive Sector, the subsequent owner of the Bendix building. This new, accessible, and verdant quadrangle location thus brings into public view a major project of renowned sculptor Nevelson.

Born in Kiev, Russia (now Ukraine), in 1899, Nevelson came to the United States with her parents in 1905 and grew up in Rockland, Maine. In 1920 she moved to New York, studied art, and slowly achieved recognition by the 1950s for her innovative sculptures. Though Nevelson initially worked almost exclusively in wood, steel became a critical medium for the artist after 1969 as she began to receive commissions for sculptures like *Trilogy* for outdoor sites.

Trilogy is composed of three elements: two vertical units that tower forty-four and thirty feet, respectively, and a single, low, ground-hugging unit that extends twelve feet in diameter. The overlapping clustering of thin, primarily geometric steel planes of the tallest component creates a comparatively sharp, precise profile, in opposition to the thirty-foot-high unit with its outward gesturing bundle of rods arcing at the top. The circular, low-lying third element in turn is composed of a miscellany of roiling, embryonic forms. While dauntingly large in scale and abstract in appearance, the black-hued *Trilogy* may nevertheless be seen as a metaphor for a trio of entities in varied stages of growth and development—or even as a family group.

B-4
Art in Detroit Receiving Hospital
and University Health Center
Detroit Receiving Hospital and University Health Center,
4201 Saint Antoine Street
1976–present

Replete with more than nine hundred art objects, from a white marble statue of Hippocrates that stands outside the entrance to a multicolored and functional suite of outdoor furnishings by George Sugarman in a courtyard adjacent to the cafeteria, the Detroit Receiving Hospital and University Health Center facilities are a major repository of public art in Detroit. Karl Apel, Harry Bertoia, Alexander Calder (see B-8), Naomi Dickerson, Marcia Freedman, Lynn Galbreath, Dick Goody, Jeff Guido, Carole Harris, Ann Healy, Richard Hunt, Lester Johnson, Robert Kidd, William King, Balthazar Korab, Janet Kuemmerlein, Charles McGee (see F-8), Glen Michaels (see F-5), Kirk Newman (see A-36d), Louise Nobili, Valerie Parks, Solomon Sekhaolelo, Robert Schefman, Vassely Ting, and George Vihos are some of the hundreds of artists represented in the collection. Moreover, a diverse array of media is showcased, from textiles, ceramics, oils, acrylics, watercolors, photography, prints, bronze, marble, and wood to mixed media installations.

From ground to top floor, from patient rooms, doctors' offices, and examining rooms to reception, lobby, and cafeteria areas, the intention of the collection is to "lighten the burden of illness of patients and families." Though not all the art here is equally accessible, several major works in the most visible areas attest to the striking vitality such an ensemble of works impart to these two institutions of the Detroit Medical Center complex.

Painter Sam Gilliam's 1980 *Wave Composition*, a vast, horizontal "painting" of mixed-media elements, stretches thirty-six feet along the main floor corridor that connects the hospital and health center. Two overlapping, paint-stained canvas panels integrated with various painted metal shapes create an active, roiling "wave composition," to cite the artist's descriptive title. The free-form, partially cut-out canvas panels mesh with several geometric metal components (circle, square, rectangle), as if to evoke the random flotsam and jetsam one might encounter in a heaving surf. The combination of horizontal sweep, rhythmic movement, vivid primary colors, materials projecting from the flat surface of the wall, and sheer size yields a work to be experienced as one either moves along the corridor or stops to view the work head-on.

Born in Mississippi in 1933, Gilliam has lived and worked in Washington, D.C., since the 1950s, where he first experimented with compositions of draped canvases. Another large-scale work by Gilliam is installed in the entrance lobby of the Patrick V. McNamara Federal Building in downtown Detroit (see A-32).

The matte green tiles that form part of ceramist Diana Pancioli's *Arc* (1996) were originally made by Detroit's Pewabic Pottery for

the Stroh Brewery Company in 1955. The tiles, which were never used, were donated by Stroh's to the Detroit People Mover (see A-37a) for use in the design of its stations. They in turn donated some of the unused tiles to Detroit Receiving Hospital and University Health Center. Pancioli then composed a design that integrated her own lustrous tiles (which constitute the center of *Arc*) with the historic Pewabic tiles. The artist, a professor at Eastern Michigan University, produced and executed this floor-to-ceiling installation (eleven by twenty-five feet) to mark the fifteenth anniversary of these cooperative institutions.

Located in the Health Center lobby opposite the main entrance, *Arc*'s radiant white, pink, and green lozenge greets all who enter. The modulation from white at its center to pink, rose, and green, as well as its circular shape, suggests a sun, star, or planet that seems to be slowly rising. Alternatively, the completion of *Arc*'s half circle in the highly reflective ceiling panels may also call to mind a segment of a rose window from a cathedral. The curvilinear outline—or arc—alludes as well to the notion of continuity, of that which draws or links together many disparate entities: people, institutions, years.

Pancioli also designed two additional murals incorporating Pewabic tile: one for the Compuware Corporation Headquarters on Campus Martius, and a two-story, three-wall installation for the Cadillac Center station of the People Mover monorail (see A-36a).

B-5
Sentry
Richard Bennett (b. 1954)
Charles H. Wright Museum of African American History,
315 East Warren Avenue at Brush Street
1996–1997
Aluminum and gold

The resplendent black and gold masks poised above the two main entrances to the Charles H. Wright Museum of African American History were fabricated by Detroiter Richard Bennett. From a considerable distance, their contrasting hues create dazzling accents, almost like flashing beacons, against the buff-colored stone structure. The mask of the Bambara people of Mali that sculptor Bennett chose as his model is notable for its slender, elongated proportions and striking headdress consisting of a row of horns that refers to the anatomy of antelopes and also resembles a comb. These masks, carved from wood, are often embellished with cowrie shells or dried berries, for which Bennett has substituted an array of gold-plated bands, diamonds, and rosettes. The multiple horns add to the decorative impact of the mask and, by linking animal and human forms, empower the wearer. At ten feet tall and four-and-a-half feet wide, Bennett's sizable visages likewise add power and majesty to the façade and mission of the museum they adorn.

B-6
The Thinker
Auguste Rodin (1840–1917)
Detroit Institute of Arts,
5200 Woodward Avenue
1880–1902 (cast 1904)
Bronze

Placed in a commanding position before the main entrance to the Detroit Institute of Arts is this cast of the famous sculpture *The Thinker* by French artist Auguste Rodin. The nude, brooding figure, hunched into a compact mass, creates a sense of total physical and mental concentration. Rodin responded to the smooth surfaces and cool images encouraged by the Beaux-Arts and academic traditions (see A-8) by modeling figures whose rough, pitted surfaces express innermost conflicts and feelings. Even though his sculptures were predominantly allegorical, they dealt courageously with the human condition in contemporary society. Describing sculpture as the art of the "bump and hollow," Rodin deliberately cultivated "unfinished" surfaces like that of *The Thinker*, allowing the play of light and shade across his works to create a greater sense of vitality and lifelike presence. Rodin first modeled *The Thinker* on a small scale, enlarging it to over-life-size around 1902. The Detroit Art Institute's cast, one of twenty-two, was the third produced by the sculptor's foundry and was presented to the museum by Horace H. Rackham in 1922. Fittingly, Rodin chose *The Thinker* to crown his own grave. Several other sculptures by Rodin may be seen in the galleries of the museum.

B-7
Gracehoper
Tony Smith (1912–1980)
Detroit Institute of Arts, Woodward Avenue at Kirby Street, North Lawn
1972
Painted steel

Gracehoper was transformed from a small work to one of monumental scale when Detroit Institute of Arts curator Samuel J. Wagstaff Jr. suggested to sculptor Tony Smith its possible enlargement for an outdoor site. Then, with the help of the Friends of Modern Art museum auxiliary group (now known as the Friends of Modern and Contemporary Art), Wagstaff secured the funds to realize the project. The successful change in scale and compatibility of the piece with the wide range of old and new buildings surrounding it is explained in part by Smith's long career as an architect, which included two years as an apprentice to Frank Lloyd Wright. In 1960, Smith turned to sculpture based on geometric solids, particularly tetrahedra, octahedra, and cubes. Painted black to emphasize its interlocking geometric sections, the house-sized *Gracehoper* measures twenty-seven feet high, twenty-three feet wide, and forty-six feet long. *Gracehoper* has an uncanny and subtle grace for so large a work. Resembling a giant insect, it was actually named after a mythical beast in James Joyce's *Finnegan's Wake*, representing dynamism, change, and progress.

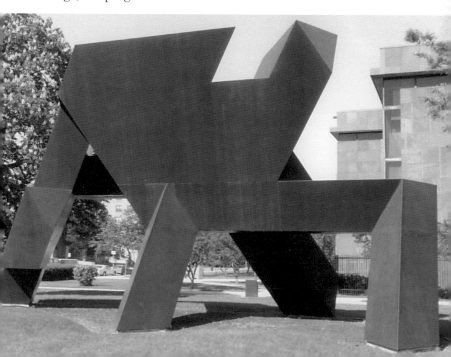

B-8
Jeune fille et sa suite (Young Woman and Her Suitors)
Alexander Calder (1898–1976)
Detroit Institute of Arts, John R and Farnsworth Streets
1970
Painted steel

For many years (1970–2006) Alexander Calder's *Jeune fille et sa suite* anchored the highly visible triangular corner in front of the AT&T building at Cass and Michigan avenues. It also twice graced the covers of the preceding editions of *Art in Detroit Public Places*, as in the photograph illustrated here. Recently AT&T presented *Jeune fille et sa suite* to the Detroit Institute of Arts, where it will be sited on the museum's grounds at John R and Farnsworth Streets in early 2008.

Calder, the inventor of moving sculpture or "mobiles" in the 1930s, later adapted the fluid, whimsical forms of his mobiles to the more monumental series of stationary works known as stabiles. Typical of Calder's witty manner, the *jeune fille*, or young lady, of the title is indicated perhaps by the tall, curvilinear shape at the center of the sculpture, suggestive of breasts or buttocks, and her suite of attendants by the more geometrical forms to either side. The twenty-ton steel sculpture was fabricated in France, where Calder lived and worked most of his life, and was assembled in Detroit.

Originally painted black at Calder's behest, *Jeune fille* was repainted "Calder red" in 1985 when the AT&T building entrance was remodeled and plantings were added. In 2007 it was returned to its original black color before its installation at the art institute. Its dark hue and curvaceous forms boldly and sensually counterpoint the sleek, white marble walls of the museum.

Two more Calders are accessible to the general public in the metropolitan area. Another stabile by the artist, *The X and Its Tails* (1967), distinguishes the entrance to the Josephine F. Ford Sculpture Garden (see B-10) on the campus of the College for Creative Studies. A colorful example of Calder's art of the mobile is suspended above the reading room of the Grosse Pointe Public Library (see C-22) and is visible from both inside and outside the building.

B-9
Curved Form with Rectangle and Space
Lois Teicher (b. 1938)
Hudson's Art Park, John R and Farnsworth Streets
2000
Stainless steel

Lois Teicher relishes the challenge of site-specific installation art. She entered a statewide competition for a sculpture for the intimately scaled Hudson's Art Park. Her winning design, *Curved Form with Rectangle and Space*, defies the constraints of the small plot of land. Blithely poised on a single corner, it rises in a graceful curve and terminates cleanly and definitively fourteen feet in the air. The dazzling white, paper-thin rectangle, fabricated of powder-coated stainless steel only an inch thick, is pierced by a narrow, asymmetrical opening that heightens the seeming weightlessness of the sculpture. Like the voids for which the English sculptors Barbara Hepworth (1903–1975) and Henry Moore (1898–1986) became famous, Teicher's opening allows the viewer to see through the form, subtly playing with negative and positive space.

The sculpture seems to pirouette in space like a dancer on toe. Humanizing geometry in this way, the artist suggests here a consonance between the concave-convex curve, with its slit-like opening, and the human body. The sculpture and the park it inhabits are the result of a collaborative effort among Hudson's Project Imagine, the City of Detroit, the Detroit Artists Market, and the University Cultural Association. Behind *Curved Form*, high on the brown brick wall of the adjacent Scarab Club, Steve Veresh's oxidized copper relief, *Phoenix*, previously installed in 1976, draws the eye further aloft.

Other public sculptures by Teicher, a graduate of the College for Creative Studies and Eastern Michigan University, are on view at Detroit's downtown Boll Family YMCA, in Mt. Clemens, Flint, and, most recently, Grand Blanc (2006).

B-10
Hip and Spine (Stone Chair Setting)
Richard Nonas (b. 1936)
Josephine F. Ford Sculpture Garden, John R and Kirby Streets
1997
Swedish granite

The Josephine F. Ford Sculpture Garden in the city's Cultural Center was made possible by a generous gift from Josephine Ford, arts patron and benefactor of the College for Creative Studies. A collaborative endeavor by the college and the Detroit Institute of Arts, the two-acre garden serves simultaneously as a campus and a sculpture park. The eleven works of art currently on display are part of the museum's permanent collection, including, among others, works by Alexander Calder, Anthony Caro, Raymond Duchamp-Villon, Michael D. Hall, Reuben Nakian, Beverly Pepper, and Richard Serra.

Richard Nonas's suite of four chairs and four tables, carved from a pinkish-gray Swedish granite, is arranged invitingly at the center of the quadrangle of grass, trees, and walkways. The massive, high-backed chairs have low, elongated seats, the better to make us aware, when seated close to the ground, of our hips and spine, as the title suggests. Trained as an anthropologist, Nonas has been known since the 1970s for his abstract geometric sculptures of wood, steel, or stone that rest directly on the floor or ground. *Hip and Spine (Stone*

Chair Setting) is an unexpectedly functional work for Nonas. The weighty grouping, with its low center of gravity, connects the sitter, through contact with the granite—one of nature's hardest, densest stones—to the solid, enduring material of the earth. The uneven, rough-hewn surfaces (only the seats are smoothly finished to provide rudimentary comfort), slanted tabletops, and short horizontal cuts along a corner or edge define this ensemble as sculpture as well as furniture conjoined in a successful union of the aesthetic and utilitarian.

The four low tables are aligned along a straight line that cuts through the conversational positioning of chairs and crosses two diagonals implied by the angles of the seats to form an intersecting design linking all eight elements into a communal whole.

Another work by Nonas, *Lucifer Landing*, on the grounds of Cranbrook (see F-18), is composed of thirty-nine boulders arranged in a Z formation on a gently sloping, grassy hillside.

B-11
Normanno Wedge I
Beverly Pepper (b. 1924)
Josephine F. Ford Sculpture Garden,
John R and Kirby Streets
1983
Cor-ten steel

Beverly Pepper's arresting *Normanno Wedge I* is one of a series she designed in which the wedge form dominates. Towering seventeen feet, the piece displays an industrial, rust-colored patina that creates a dramatic counterpoint, rather like an exclamation point, to the variegated buildings and multihued sculptures behind and around it. *Normanno Wedge* consists of three divergent shapes: the tall, thin wedge bears down on and seems to bisect a nut- or keyhole-like square supported by a truncated, conical base. The opposition of the downward movement of the massive wedge, the spliced and punctured square, and the sturdy if truncated cone sets in motion the basic tensions of the piece.

According to Pepper, the title refers to the Norman invasion of Italy during medieval times. The powerful changes brought about by invading forces may be compared to the sundering action of the wedge (along with the square and cone's instinctive resistance). The wedge-shaped chisel is also used by sculptors and builders to shape wood, marble, and stone. Pepper, born in Brooklyn, New York, has lived and worked since 1951 in Rome, the capital city of a country with a long historical tradition of architectural sculpture.

B-12
Patterns of Detroit
Hubert Massey (b. 1958) and various artists
College for Creative Studies, Parking Structure,
East Wall, Brush Street between Frederick Douglass
and Ferry Streets
2001–2005
Glazed tile

The *Patterns of Detroit* Community Mural Project began in the fall of 2001, when the decision was made to enhance the new parking structure of the College for Creative Studies (CCS) by decorating the long brick and concrete wall that faces Peck Park across the street from the school's campus. To oversee the process, an advisory

committee was formed with representatives from several Cultural Center institutions and the Art Center Citizens' District Council.

As completed in 2005, *Patterns of Detroit* features a three-story central panel designed by Hubert Massey and seventeen side panels, each five by fifteen feet, arranged along three horizontal bands extending from each side of Massey's composition. Executed in glazed ceramic tile, Massey's boldly delineated and vibrantly colored image depicts a haloed mother and her child framed by significant neighborhood landmarks. Cradling her youngster, the "mother of civilization" (according to Massey) sews a fabric of colorful patterns that represent the heterogeneous cultures of Detroit. Winding through the central image, the textile seems to be echoed by the horizontal panels, transforming the parking structure into a massive brick and tile "crazy quilt."

Massey, a Detroit artist with a dossier of muralistic projects, has executed works for the Charles H. Wright Museum of African American History, Atheneum Hotel, Detroit Athletic Club, and Internal Revenue Service (see A-31). A number of youth and school groups created the multifarious designs of the flanking panels. Each group was led by a practicing artist from the community, including, among others, Sabrina Nelson, Dennis Orlowski (C-24), Kathleen Rashid, Gilda Snowden, and Vito Valdez (D-13). Youth interns at the college, under the direction of Tom Phardel, professor of ceramics, converted the sketches into ceramic tile. In the process, they discovered formulas and techniques to extend the longevity of tile exposed to weather. The completed installation is a blend of multicolored glazed tiles—whole, cut and pieced, and broken to form tesserae. *Patterns of Detroit* rewards both near and long-range viewing of its tile components and its striking, large-scale decorative forms. Notably, as Mikel Bresee, the CCS Community Arts Partnerships director, has pointed out, vacant spaces on the wall remain available so that the work can be expanded in the future. Another collaborative art project, *"Connections" Bridge* (2004), is on view in Peck Park.

B-13
Arch: Montrose
Susanna Linburg (b. 1935)
College for Creative Studies, Ferry and John R Streets
1991
Painted steel

Susanna Linburg's *Arch: Montrose* is one of a series of sculptures begun in the early 1980s that incorporate the arch as a primary motif. For Linburg, such structures are both architectural (reminiscent of the rounded arches of Roman buildings) and a reference to woman as architecture (legs surmounted by the sensuous curves of the torso above). In this variation it seems as though the several gently curving segments are about to float free, exploding and lifting off from the supporting columns. These portals imply both enclosure and openness; the vertical supports embody that which is formal and geometric, while the multiple arches allude to the spontaneous and gestural. *Montrose* serves as an appropriate symbol for the heady experience of discovery and creativity at the College for Creative Studies, and

its cobalt blue color evokes as well the expansiveness of the sky. The subtitle refers to a small town in Colorado where the sculptor's father lived.

Relocated in 2005 to a fenced-in recess between the college's admissions and administrations buildings, the metaphorical import of *Arch* has been to some degree compromised.

Born in Indiana, Linburg studied at the Slade School of Art, London, and Wayne State University. She taught art at the College for Creative Studies from 1963 to 1991.

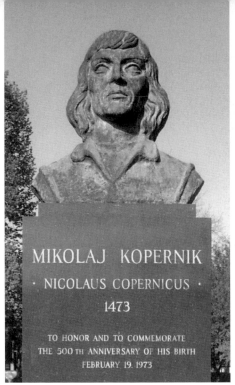

B-14
Mikolaj Kopernik (Nicolaus Copernicus)
Ferenc Varga (1906–1989)
Detroit Public Library, Woodward Avenue at Kirby Street, Lawn
1973
Bronze and granite

This representation of the famed Polish astronomer Mikolaj Kopernik (1473–1543), popularly known as Copernicus, was modeled by Hungarian-born Ferenc Varga, who was also responsible for the statue on Washington Boulevard of the Polish-born American Revolutionary War hero General Casimir Pulaski. Commemorating the five hundredth anniversary of the birth of Copernicus, the memorial was presented to the City of Detroit by the Copernicus Observances Committee, Inc. Varga chose to depict the astronomer as a youth, stressing his prominent nose and sunken cheekbones to convey an arresting and intense personality. Varga's son Frank (b. 1943) executed a mosaic portrait of Copernicus above the entrance to the library's Catalogue Department and a bronze statue of General Alexander Macomb in downtown Mt. Clemens (see E-5).

B-15
The River of Knowledge
Millard Sheets (1907–1989)
Detroit Public Library, Cass Avenue Entrance
1963
Mosaic

The Cass Avenue entrance to the addition to the Detroit Public Library (1958–1963) is set off from flanking white marble façades by its dark green marble, red mosaic columns, and the sixteen-by-forty-two-foot mosaic designed by California artist Millard Sheets. Made possible by the Edwin Austin Abbey Memorial Trust Fund for mural painting in the United States, this richly colored glass mosaic depicts, to paraphrase the inscription running the length of the work, the river of knowledge that unites past and present, a river from which all may drink and be refreshed. The mosaic was conceived in five sections, to conform to the architectural divisions of the entrance created by the red mosaic pillars, and illustrates, with images accompanied by scholarly quotations, various beneficial effects of knowledge, such as strength, the ordering of chaos, foresight, and perspective. The central panel shows a family whose search for knowledge is rewarded by a greater sense of harmony with the universe.

B-16
Exploration
Joseph N. DeLauro (1916–2006)
Detroit Public Library, Cass Avenue Entrance
1967
Bronze

Exploration by Joseph N. DeLauro is an appropriately titled sculpture for its location adjacent to an entrance to the Detroit Public Library. It is one of a trio of thematically related artworks about discovery that grace the exterior of the city's central library building. A bust of the astronomer Copernicus (B-14) and a mural titled *The River of Knowledge* (B-15) complete the grouping.

As if caught in mid-movement, DeLauro's figure, garbed in a full-length, voluminous gown, draws back her torso, thrusts out one knee, and sweeps her long skirt into a crescent-like shape. The circle formed by the skirt is rhymed by the delicate "sighting" or "framing" circle she makes with the fingers of her other hand. The figure's gravity-defying pose and asymmetric silhouette are accentuated by the two braids of hair that project from her head. This personification of "exploration," poised at the entrance to the library, signals the kind of exhilaration that awaits the visitor to such repositories of knowledge.

Born in Connecticut, DeLauro studied at Yale University and the University of Iowa before settling in the Midwest, where he taught at Detroit's Marygrove College, the University of Detroit Mercy, and the University of Windsor, Canada.

Marquette, LaSalle, Cadillac, and Richard

Julius T. Melchers (1829–1908)
Wayne State University, Ludington Plaza,
Anthony Wayne Drive between West Warren Avenue
and Merrick Street
1874 (installed this location 1974)
Sandstone

Several years after the completion in 1871 of Detroit's new city hall, art patron Bela Hubbard (1814–1896), who had made a fortune in lumber and real estate, presented to the city four statues to fill the empty niches of the façade. Julius T. Melchers, Detroit's first

sculptor, carved the larger-than-life figures of the four French pioneers who helped open up the Territory of Michigan and establish the city of Detroit. The statue of Marquette (*far left*) was carved by Melchers after a model created by architect John M. Donaldson (1854–1941). Rescued from their niches when city hall was demolished in 1960–1961, the statues were stored for a number of years until the Detroit Common Council presented them to Wayne State University, where they were installed in 1974. Here, displayed at different heights and in an asymmetric design of pedestals, plantings, and walls, the imposing quartet can now be seen fully in the round in an informal, park-like setting, thanks to the generosity of the Ludington family of Detroit.

B-18
Untitled
Ed Sykes (b. 1970)
Wayne State University, Anthony Wayne Drive and West Warren Avenue
2001
Stainless steel

Untitled, a shiny, reflective sculpture that dominates a corner site on the grounds of Wayne State University, honors Andrzej W. Olbrot, a professor who was slain by a student in a campus classroom in 1998. Born in Poland, Olbrot taught computer engineering at Wayne for a decade. After his tragic death, members of the College of Engineering raised funds from faculty, students, friends, and members of Detroit's large Polish community to commission an original work of art in his memory.

Ed Sykes's proposal for a form dramatically cantilevered into space, supported only by two cylindrical struts at one end, embodies Olbrot's pioneering research in computer time-delay systems. As the artist has stated, the bulbous organic spheres in various stages of formation, combined with a slender, slightly angled, horizontal "spire," symbolize "two systems—art and engineering." The organic spheres suggest shapes in the process of development (akin perhaps to creative ideas bubbling forth in the mind) that generate technological breakthroughs—whether a spire or measuring tools that engineers and designers invent. Thirteen feet wide and seven feet high, *Untitled* parallels the ground, in contrast to the perpendicular orientation of many memorials, and echoes but does not compete with the sweeping curve of the façade of the Engineering Department building before which it stands.

When the piece was installed, its polished, mirror-like surface was deemed too glossy; against the artist's wishes, it was sanded to soften the glare of its reflective skin. Sykes, who studied at Lawrence Technological University in Southfield, Michigan, now makes his home in Oakland, California.

B-19
Helios Trail

Bruce White (b. 1933)
Wayne State University,
College of Engineering, Warren Avenue
and Anthony Wayne Drive
1989
Stainless steel

This forty-foot-tall piece, according to sculptor Bruce White, refers to the sun god Helios "lighting the sky, creating a blaze of light." Composed of two tapering shafts joined together to form a "V" shape and fabricated from both polished and brushed stainless steel, *Helios Trail* thrusts up in front of the Wayne State University College of Engineering. Mounted on a low, triangular, stepped plinth of black concrete, the slim, silvery form, like a flash of light, symbolizes the questing, experimental character of the engineering discipline. As the sleek blade pushes upward, it appears to leave a jagged, flame-like trail in its wake. Formally, the angular, dynamic momentum of the narrowing shape is heightened by virtue of its contrast with the emphatically horizontal lines and brown brick of the surrounding buildings.

A professor at Northern Illinois University, sculptor White was awarded the commission for *Helios Trail* in a national competition sponsored by the College of Engineering. This successful collaboration between engineering and art suggests the sometimes overlooked but strong ties that exist between these interdependent disciplines.

B-20
Continuity
Jayson D. Lowery (b. 1976)
Wayne State University, Gullen Mall at West Warren and Second Avenue
2004
Marble and steel

Donated by the Wayne State University Alumni Association, *Continuity* is the centerpiece of an intimate, semi-enclosed commemorative garden honoring Thomas N. Bonner, who served as the seventh president of the university from 1978 to 1982. Bonner's role as president is noted on the commemorative plaque, but equally important, according to sculptor Jayson D. Lowery, was his teaching career at Wayne as a medical historian (1982–1997) following his presidential tenure. Lowery's interpretation of "continuity"—that timeworn ideas and images often lie at the core of modern endeavors—is central to this memorial, for it is mentors like Bonner who serve as vital links in the transmission of knowledge to new generations of students.

For *Continuity* the sculptor chose a six-foot block of marble, the quintessential medium of classical statuary. Into two faces of its smooth, monolithic form he carved one-half of an elliptical niche, softly texturing the inner surfaces. When viewed on a diagonal—from the work's "front" corner—the double recesses read as a Gothic arch evoking sacred medieval architecture and hushed spiritual settings meant for contemplation. On the other side, two rust-colored plates, each cut to form half of a pointed arch, encase the stone, likewise invoking a Gothic vocabulary. The somewhat harsh juxtaposition of steel and marble—the first a modern industrial product and the second with its classical allusions—is yet another manifestation of the not-always-smooth continuum of the old into the new.

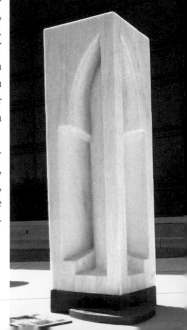

Lowery, an Arizona native, studied at Northern Arizona University, Flagstaff, and Wayne State University, where he taught for several years. Since 2006 he has lived and worked in Newport, Oregon.

B-21
Automotive Mural
William Gropper (1897–1977)
Wayne State University, Student Center Building, Gullen Mall
1941
Oil on canvas

This six-by-forty-foot mural was originally installed in two sections at opposite ends of the lobby of the Northwestern Branch Post Office at Joy Road and Grand River Avenue, and funded by the U.S. Treasury. William Gropper was a social-realist painter perhaps best known for his satirical political cartoons. Indeed, he said that because of his radical politics he was denied entry into automotive plants for research or to sketch and draw, and hence he was forced to take his imagery largely from photographs in *Life* magazine.

Notably, in *Automotive Mural* Gropper tackled the same subject as depicted in the famed *Detroit Industry* frescoes completed seven years earlier by Mexican muralist Diego Rivera (1886–1957) in the Detroit Institute of Arts. In choosing to render in the right panel the production of the various parts of an automobile and on the left the final assembly of the automobile, Gropper was clearly influenced by the Mexican's Detroit murals. While Rivera's ambitious frescoes confront the meaning of the technological age for human life, Gropper focused on a celebration of the power of labor. His idealized, Atlas-like workers vigorously perform their various tasks. The alternation of large foreground figures with small background figures creates a lively rhythm across the composition. The murals were removed from the post office before its demolition in 1971 and recombined in the Wayne State University Student Center Building. They were a gift to the university from the National Collection of Fine Arts, Washington, D.C., and their reinstallation, which Gropper professed to be delighted with, was made possible by a grant from the National Endowment for the Arts.

B-22
Wings of Learning
G. Alden Smith (1912–1993)
Wayne State University,
Mort Harris Recreation and
Fitness Center, Gullen Mall
1965
Brass and steel

This dramatic, sixteen-foot-high work was commissioned by the Wayne State University graduating class of 1962 from G. Alden Smith, long-time chairperson (1960–1977) of Wayne's art and art history department. Educated at the School of the Art Institute of Chicago, Smith worked in a variety of media, including steel, bronze, Plexiglas, and wood. Here, composing in brass and steel, Smith divided nine carved blades into three levels, one merging into another and finally bursting open at the top, abstractly visualizing the process of learning. Formerly located in the open air, *Wings of Learning* was reinstalled (2000) on the north side of the Mort Harris Recreation and Fitness Center where the sculpture's airy, sweeping silhouette feels constrained by a semi-enclosed, roofed-over "porch."

B-23
General Anthony Wayne
Sergio De Giusti (b. 1941)
Wayne State University,
Centennial Courtyard,
Gullen and Reuther Malls
1969
Bronze, granite, and marble

This tribute to General Anthony Wayne by Sergio De Giusti was commissioned by the Wayne State University Alumni Association to mark the centennial of the origin of the university in 1868. The impetuous "Mad Anthony Wayne," after whom the university was named in 1933, distinguished himself during the Revolutionary War and at the battle of Fallen Timbers (1794) near Toledo, Ohio. There, he defeated a force of Native Americans in a battle that paved the way for the then nascent American government to take possession of Detroit from the British two years later.

In this circular relief portrait, the general's head and shoulders emerge from a dark bronze background. His unruly hair, bushy eyebrows, and nose project prominently, while his down-turned mouth, squinting eyes, and hunched shoulders convey the aura of a powerful, fearsome individual. Epaulets and lapels of his coat also push forward, adding to his intimidating presence. The tondo shape, often associated with religious paintings or formal portraits of the Italian Renaissance, is about three feet in diameter. It rests on a three-foot-high pedestal, with the result that a visitor to the circular centennial courtyard meets the "mad" general eye to eye. The reverse side of the bronze disc fittingly replicates the 1968 Wayne State University centennial symbol designed by Richard Bilaitis, a professor in the Art Department at the time.

Sculptor De Giusti, born in Italy, arrived in Detroit in 1954. Since completing his studies at Wayne State University in 1968, he has taught, curated exhibitions, and executed numerous sculptural commissions in the region. See also A-14 and A-22.

B-24

Midmien

Sasson Soffer (b. 1925)
Wayne State University, Community Arts Building, Reuther Mall,
Cass Avenue at West Kirby Street
1978
Stainless steel

Poised weightlessly on a gently sloping, grassy lawn near the entrance to the Community Arts Building on Wayne State University's campus, the double rings of Sasson Soffer's *Midmien* form a kind of continuous line drawing in space. Without a perceivable beginning or ending, the silvery flow of curving lines conveys, largely as a result of the symmetrical contours, a kind of calm midpoint or equilibrium, as if rolling hoops had stopped in mid-revolution. The Iraqi-born sculptor, who lives in New York, fabricated a twin to *Midmien,* and both were on view on Wayne's campus for a time in 1978. Subsequently, *Midmien*'s sibling, titled *Mien,* was moved to New York.

The graceful arcs and expansive sweep of the sixteen-foot-tall circles of *Midmien,* along with a circle's connotations of continuity and infinity, aptly embody the ongoing life of the visual arts taught, studied, and displayed in this university building. *Midmien* was a gift to Wayne State from area patron-collectors Lila and Gilbert Silverman.

B-25
Nymph and Faun
Giacomo Manzu (1908–1991)
Wayne State University, McGregor Memorial Sculpture Garden, Gullen Mall
1968
Bronze and marble

Nymph and Faun, the second of Giacomo Manzu's two Detroit sculptures, was commissioned by architect Minoru Yamasaki (1912–1986) for the McGregor Memorial Sculpture Garden at Wayne State University. For the expansive, sunken, semi-secluded site on the university's campus, in contrast to the solitary *Passo di Danza* (A-25) fronting on busy Jefferson Avenue downtown, Manzu conceived a two-figure composition.

Throughout his career, Manzu was committed to the depiction of the human form, which is perhaps best seen in his many casts of female figures. Presented in simple, unaffected poses, they are shown dancing, arranging their hair, sitting quietly on a chair, or, as here, reclining. Though based on a mythological subject, the encounter between nymph and crouching faun is unaffectedly natural. The nymph wears a short slip or shift, while the faun is nude. Except for his over-large ears, the curious faun (sometimes represented as part animal) is human in form. Apparently his presence has just been sensed by the nymph, who raises her head and upper body in response. The naturalism of the figures is further reinforced by the noticeable, albeit understated, surface texture that renders visible the hand of the artist.

The over-life-size figures (the nymph stretches out to a length of nine feet), joined together on a broad, six-by-eighteen-foot marble plinth, echo in their ground-hugging profiles the calm, contemplative atmosphere of the Japanese rock and water garden for which they were conceived. *Nymph and Faun* was a gift of the McGregor Fund in honor of the university's centennial in 1968.

B-26
Nordkyn
Robert Murray (b. 1936)
Wayne State University, Ferry Mall, Cass Avenue at West Ferry Street
1974
Painted steel

Canadian sculptor Robert Murray was commissioned by Detroit collector and patron W. Hawkins Ferry (1914–1988) to design this piece for the Ferry Mall, a plaza on the Wayne State University campus financed by the Dexter M. Ferry Jr. Trustee Corporation. Murray created *Nordkyn* (named after an island in Lake Huron) from a single sheet of three-quarter-inch steel. Although clearly made of metal, the sculpture resembles a gigantic folded-paper construction because of the thinness of the steel and the creases and splits of the surface. *Nordkyn,* anchored at only three points, is stabilized through a subtle manipulation of the planes into a system of checks and balances. The deep, brilliant, royal blue color of the sculpture increases the sense of lightness and enlivens this outdoor space, surrounded by the utilitarian materials, concrete, tile, and brick, and the muted colors of this urban university setting. Originally poised directly on the pavement, *Nordkyn* now sits on an overscaled marble base elevated above the ground.

B-27
Silverbolt (Detroit Horse Power IV)
John Kearney (b. 1924)
Children's Museum, 6134 Second Avenue
1972
Chrome-plated steel

Nebraska-born John Kearney studied sculpture at the Cranbrook Academy of Art and in Perugia, Italy. Now living and working in Chicago, Kearney has fashioned innumerable sculptures of animals using American industrial materials. Here, the shiny, spirited horse that commands the entrance to the Children's Museum has been molded out of automobile bumpers. Using an acetylene torch, hammer, and file, Kearney created the eight-foot-tall, chrome-plated *Silverbolt*.

Often intended as a symbol of strength and dominance, the horse figures prominently as subject matter in sculpture, from the life-size ceramic horses (c. 220–206 BC) excavated from the tomb of the Chinese emperor, Shi Huangdi, to the anxious equestrians of the twentieth-century Italian, Marino Marini. Kearney's steed, ironically, has been made from the very materials of the invention that marked the demise of the horse as a mode of transportation. Indeed, funds for *Silverbolt* were provided by several Detroit automotive companies.

B-28
An American Lightbow and Jennifer's Butterfly
S. Thomas Scarff (b. 1942)
New Center One, 3031 West Grand Boulevard
and Second Avenue, Atrium
1983
Aluminum, neon tubing, and steel cable

An American Lightbow and *Jennifer's Butterfly* by S. Thomas Scarff
are dramatically suspended from the ceiling of the ten-story atrium
of the New Center One retail and office building. The two hanging
constructions are an intriguing amalgam of the semi-recognizable
and fantastic. The colored neon tubes that highlight edges not only
differentiate them from the surrounding architecture but also lend a

futuristic glow. The titles, however, help identify the actual sources of sculptor Scarff's imagery—eagles that fly like arrows (*American Lightbow*) and a butterfly. While neither sculpture is precise in its anatomical details, the sleek, curved body of an eagle and the wing-like extensions of a butterfly are identifiable. Although they are weighty structures (upward of one thousand pounds) that each measure fifty to sixty feet in height, in the vast, airy space of the atrium they serve as metaphors of flight and movement. Their placement, on either side of an elevator shaft that rises through the middle of the aviary-like space, sets off the opposing natures of these airborne creatures: the aerodynamic eagle and the fluttering butterfly.

Born in Iowa, Scarff studied at the School of the Art Institute of Chicago and currently lives and works in Chicago.

B-29
Continuity Tower
Robert Sestok (b. 1946)
West Grand Boulevard and Third Street, Median
1990
Steel

Continuity Tower, an airy, see-through columnar structure, celebrates, according to its accompanying plaque, "the memory of Jacqueline Feigenson who saw most clearly that art begins with artists." Feigenson (1934–1984) was a dedicated gallery owner in Detroit who exhibited primarily avant-garde regional artists, including Detroit-based Robert Sestok. Sestok was commissioned in 1990 to construct a memorial to the late dealer.

Sestok, like a number of his Detroit contemporaries, works with found objects gleaned from the city, with which he builds freestanding or wall-hung assemblages. In *Continuity Tower*, myriad diverse steel fragments, some flat and smooth, some curved or textured, along with steel I-, H-, and L-shaped elements, have been welded to a twelve-foot-tall framework. In the process of construction, such a tower accumulates more and more parts as it rises, seemingly bound for infinity, as the title implies. Near the top, two recognizable shapes are visible: a human profile purposefully gazing outward and a partial figure of a child, alluding perhaps to the children who will achieve goals in the future.

Aligned with a row of trees that landscape the median of this busy boulevard, *Continuity Tower*'s lean, ventilated shape and dark brown patina blend perhaps a little too fluently with the tree trunks, making this tower somewhat difficult to locate initially. A related but later cylindrical sculpture by Sestok occupies a spacious downtown location (A-14) and a wall painting by the artist, who also works two-dimensionally, animates an industrial riverfront site (D-15).

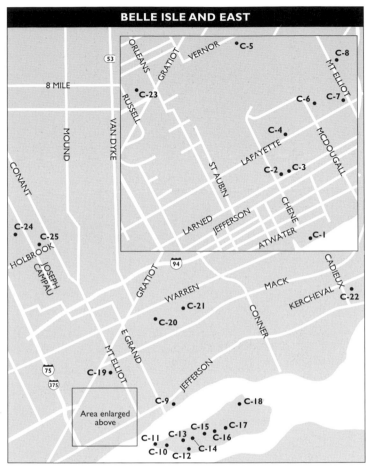

BELLE ISLE AND EAST

C-1. The Carnival!
C-2. Untitled
C-3. Fanfare
C-4. Renaissance Rebirth
C-5. The Dance of Life
C-6. Waterman Monument (Flight of the Spirit)
C-7. Covenant
C-8. Creation Garden
C-9. Father Gabriel Richard
C-10. James Scott Memorial Fountain
C-11. Untitled
C-12. Levi L. Barbour Memorial Fountain
C-13. Spanish-American War Monument

C-14. James J. Brady Memorial
C-15. Major General Alpheus Starkey Williams
C-16. Johann Friedrich von Schiller
C-17. Dante Alighieri
C-18. Gazelle
C-19. Heidelberg Project
C-20. ABZ–Everything Is Anything
C-21. Untitled
C-22. Salute to Knowledge
C-23. Eastern Market Murals
C-24. Pope John Paul II
C-25. History of Poland

C. Belle Isle and East

C-1
The Carnival!
John Piet (b. 1946)
Chene Park, Atwater Street
between Chene and
Dubois Streets
1984, reconstructed 1991
Painted steel

This trio of colorful, animated forms perched on the bank of the Detroit River looks like an impromptu gathering of street (or park) performers. Vivid red, blue, and green shapes can readily be associated with the gestural movements of clowns, stilt-walkers, jugglers, or trained animals at a carnival. As one circles the piece, the components seem to twist, turn, and revolve, shifting and regrouping as they alternately incline toward or away from one another. Although they are set within a circular arena, the absence of a pedestal places them on the same level as the observers, while the see-through, skeletal armatures of each humanizes them despite their twelve-, eighteen-, and twenty-foot heights.

John Piet is well represented in private and public collections in the Detroit metropolitan area; works by the sculptor are also on view in Harmonie and Pingree parks (A-11, C-20). *The Carnival!* is one of three sculptures commissioned by the Detroit Recreation Department in 1984 for this riverfront site. Sculptures by Ray Katz (see E-10) and Richard Tucker have also been sensitively integrated into various locations in Chene Park.

Damaged by an errant automobile in 1990, *The Carnival!* was reconstructed the following year.

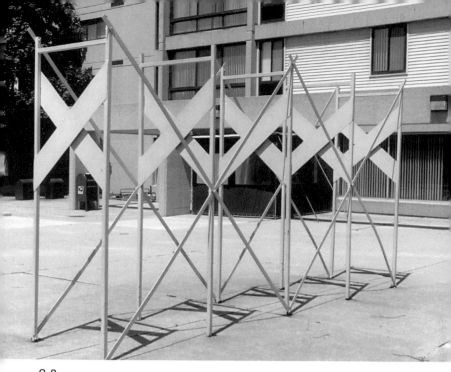

C-2
Untitled
John Gregory McCarthy (b. 1948)
Elmwood Park Plaza, East Larned and Chene Streets
1974
Painted steel

A colorful signal to the entrance of the sculpture-filled Elmwood Park Plaza, this bright yellow sculpture by Illinois-born John Gregory McCarthy, who studied at the University of Arizona and at the Cranbrook Academy of Art, at first glance resembles a scaffold. A second look reveals that the vertical steel struts and cross-members are in fact too thin to support very much weight. Rather, the piece is airy and delicate in feeling, despite its considerable size (eight feet six inches by sixteen feet by three feet). From the side, five broad X-shaped forms become visible. Repeating each other in parallel succession, they resemble festive banners, their sunny yellow color adding a cheerful note to the concrete court. A heftier but less colorful example of McCarthy's abstract art is installed at the northern terminus of Washington Boulevard in downtown Detroit.

A modestly scaled sculpture by Stanley Dolega (see C-11) is also situated in this plaza. Dolega's, McCarthy's, and David Stoltz's (C-3) works are all on extended loan from the collection of Gilbert and Lila Silverman.

C-3
Fanfare
David Stoltz (b. 1943)
Elmwood Park Plaza, East Larned and Chene Streets
1974
Steel

At the far end of the Elmwood Park Plaza court, opposite the sculpture by John Gregory McCarthy (C-2), stands *Fanfare*, a compact
piece by Brooklyn–born sculptor David Stoltz, who studied at the
Pratt Institute. Measuring six by ten by six feet, it rests before a row
of trees, behind which rises a one-story brick wall. Made of four
joined steel bands of uniform thickness, *Fanfare* appears to open toward the viewer like a pleated fan—or the loud flourish of a brass
band. Thus, Stoltz's folding, bending, and twisting of steel imbue
this rigid material with energy and supple movement. A more extensive and complex work by Stoltz, *Steel V* (1975), consisting of bent
steel bands spread across the floor in piles several layers deep, is in
the Detroit Institute of Arts. Since the mid-1980s, Stoltz has created
sculpture in a semi-figurative vein—a large, populous ensemble
called *Carousel* is a current long-term undertaking—and now lives
and works in Miami, Florida.

C-4
Renaissance Rebirth
James Nani (b. 1926)
East Lafayette Boulevard between Chene and McDougall Streets
1980
Cor-ten steel

Renaissance Rebirth, a tall, curvaceous sculpture by area artist James Nani, stands at the entrance to the Parkview Square apartments. Nani, born in New York, studied with sculptor Alexander Archipenko (1887–1964) and later at Wayne State University. He was commissioned by the City of Detroit in 1979 to develop a sculpture for this apartment complex, then one of several being built east of downtown.

Made of Cor-ten steel, and centered on a low rise of ground on a semicircular traffic island, *Renaissance Rebirth* twists and turns as it rises eighteen feet into the air. Despite its large size and the thickness of steel, it reads like a ribbon or Möbius strip of curves and reverse curves formed from a supple, pliant material—like a line drawn in space. Its open, spiraling form, appearing to move upward above a stabilizing cylindrical pedestal, and its abstract shape fittingly represent the renewal of a part of the city that has now been filled in with parks, apartment buildings, and townhouses.

C-5
The Dance of Life
Ann F. Smith (b. 1960)
McDonald Square Condominiums, 2301 Prince Hall Drive,
South of East Vernor Highway
1983
Cor-ten steel

Detroiter Ann F. Smith, a longtime devotee of dance, studied art at the College for Creative Studies with sculptor Susanna Linburg (see B-13). These interests are combined in *The Dance of Life*, a Cor-ten steel sculpture erected by the Elmwood III Citizens District Council. Five androgynous performers stretch and gesture in multiple directions, yet all are linked by hand-to-hand contact. Especially notable is the straight-backed figure seated in the center, whom the artist describes as an "embodiment of strength," poised to rise and join the others. These life-size figures nimbly and vigorously enact the rhythmic rise and fall of the age-old dance of life. As in a painting, the dancers are flattened and silhouetted within a gigantic frame (six-and-a-half by eighteen feet) that momentarily freezes them within the infinitely larger sphere of three-dimensional space we all inhabit. A related motif informs Oscar Stonerov's frieze of dancers on the campus of Wayne State University on Cass Avenue at Kirby Street.

C-6
Waterman Monument (Flight of the Spirit)
Randolph Rogers (1825–1892)
Elmwood Cemetery, 1200 Elmwood Avenue, Section F
1868
Marble

This elegant memorial, commissioned by J. W. Waterman for his family in 1867 from Randolph Rogers, is one of this sculptor's rare carvings in low relief. Under an arch incised onto a simple, elegant stone shaft, or stele, a nearly life-size veiled female swathed in cling-

ing drapery, her arms folded across her chest in supplication, floats ethereally across the surface, a poignant image of the departure of the soul. The gravestone is capped by a pediment whose elegant volutes evoke in reverse the swirling drapery of the figure below. Carved in Carrara marble, the relief was executed by Rogers in Rome and shows the personal side of the sculptor responsible for such public monuments as *Michigan Soldiers and Sailors* in downtown Detroit (A-1). Rogers later used *Flight of the Spirit* for his own family tomb in Campo Verano, Rome.

A number of other marble sculptures by Rogers are part of the collection of the Detroit Institute of Arts.

C-7
Covenant
Hugh Timlin (b. 1945)
Mt. Elliott Cemetery,
1701 Mt. Elliott Street,
Southeast Section/Quadrant
1988
Marble

The six-foot-tall *Covenant* is dedicated to the memory of Tim and Kathy Crowley, teenage siblings who succumbed to cystic fibrosis, to this day an incurable disease. To remember them and simultaneously assert a measure of hope and resistance to loss and death, Hugh Timlin designed an elegant memorial whose contemplative character is reflected in the artist's choice of a white marble with soft gray veining.

The two square, tapering columns that rise unembellished from the base deftly interlock at the top in a gesture that evokes filial affection. The apparently gender-neutral forms each embrace and receive the other. *Covenant*, a title Timlin has employed for other sculptures composed of separate but linked parts, may refer to an aesthetic conjoining of discrete elements to create a whole, to ties between sister and brother, to commitments between a diety and humanity, or, here, to the implicit pledge of the living to find a cure for a deadly disease. *Covenant* is also ultimately an assertion of remembrance, affirmation, and fecundity countering the specter of death.

Evocative, in its stark simplicity, of the art of the Romanian Constantin Brancusi (1876–1957), *Covenant* likewise reveals Timlin's attachment to the columnar forms of Midwestern grain elevators and the pillared temples of religious architectural spaces. A native Detroiter, Timlin has taught at the College for Creative Studies (where he also studied) and Wayne State University. He lives and works near Mt. Pleasant, Michigan.

C-8
Creation Garden
Various artists
Solanus Casey Center, 1780 Mt. Elliott Street
2002
Various media

This oasis of calm and quiet, just east of downtown Detroit, is part of the pilgrimage center named after Capuchin friar Solanus Casey, who ministered to the hungry, troubled, and ill while serving at St. Bonaventure Church and Monastery from 1924 to 1945. *Creation Garden* is designed in the traditional architectural style of a cloister: a square, open space enclosed on its perimeters by a covered walkway. Here, however, the side fronting busy Mt. Elliott Street was left open to extend an invitation to enter and to create a view into the cloister's plantings and sculptures even when the entrance gate is closed on occasion.

Within the garden, seven modestly scaled sculptures conceived by artists of diverse racial, ethnic, religious, and cultural backgrounds are sited along a curving pathway. The layout and theme of this edenic setting derive from Saint Francis of Assisi's canticle "Brother Sun, Sister Moon," in which nature's creative forces are personified in the guise of brothers and sisters: Brother Sun, Sister Earth, Brother Fire, Sister Water, and so on. Hashim al-Tawil visualized *Sister Water* as a monolith whose surface, covered with glistening yellow and blue tiles, bears a quotation in Arabic script from the Koran praising water as a symbol of mercy and forgiveness. Johnny Bear Contreras's *Sister Earth* represents a curvaceous woman who appears to emerge from the soil. Nancy Frankel's caststone *Sister Moon*, fashioned of interlocking circular elements, summons up the moon's phases.

This haven for reflection and meditation is just one of many community-minded outreach efforts of the Capuchin Order, which is well-known in Detroit for its soup kitchen that has fed many of the city's needy for over seventy years.

C-9
Father Gabriel Richard
Leonard D. Jungwirth (1903–1963)
Gabriel Richard Park, East Jefferson Avenue
and Sheridan Street
1937–1940
Granite

Father Gabriel Richard (1767–1832), a young Sulpician priest, made important contributions to the early spiritual, educational, and cultural life of Detroit. Arriving here in June 1798, he became pastor of Saint Anne's (Detroit's first parish church) in 1802. In the following years, he published Detroit's first newspaper, established churches and schools (including the University of Michigan, which he cofounded), and was elected to Congress. He died while ministering to the ill during a cholera epidemic. To portray Father Richard's unceasing dedication, sculptor Leonard Jungwirth presented him standing firmly on a pedestal, a book clutched in his left hand, his gaze and jaw resolutely set. Choosing granite for both figure and pedestal, Jungwirth heightened the impact of the whole by eliminating detail and carving the figure in smooth, broad planes to convey the strength and purpose of character of this pioneering priest. The stiff, block-like quality of the work, recalling the original slab of granite from which it was carved, reflects an aesthetic approach to sculpture, common in the 1920s and 1930s, which advocated direct carving of the stone instead of modeling a figure in clay or plaster for later translation into bronze or marble. The execution of the heroic, thirteen-foot-high figure and three-foot-high pedestal was sponsored by the Works Progress Administration Federal Arts Project. Born in Detroit, Jungwirth taught for many years at Michigan State University, where he also carved an image of the larger-than-life Spartan, the symbol of the university.

Father Richard is also memorialized on one of the pylons adjacent to the UAW-Ford Center (A-27) and in a statue by Julius Melchers now installed on the campus of Wayne State University (B-17).

C-10
James Scott Memorial Fountain
Cass Gilbert (1859–1954) and Herbert Adams (1858–1945)
Belle Isle, Western End
1925
Marble, bronze, and tile

James Scott (1831–1910) was a somewhat shady, eccentric, and highly controversial figure in Detroit's history. When he died, leaving the city approximately $500,000 to erect a fountain on Belle Isle, his dubious character caused public resistance to carrying out his wishes for celebrating his memory. But eventually the city accepted

his gift. A competition was held in 1914, and New York architect Cass Gilbert (who the next year was named architect for the Detroit Public Library) was selected to design the fountain. He in turn recommended Herbert Adams, also of New York, to execute the portrait statue of James Scott. To accommodate the elaborate fountain and extensive reflecting lagoon, the western end of the island was extended a thousand yards. Gracefully integrated into the landscape and lavishly decorated in the true Beaux-Arts tradition (see A-8), the fountain rises gradually in three levels from a lagoon to a central column of water capable of shooting seventy-five feet into the air. Myriad jets of water spout playfully from the mouths of dolphins, lions, turtles, Neptune figures, and drinking horns. The broad basin of the reflecting pool is lined with a border and decorative medallions from Detroit's Pewabic Pottery representing seahorses, crabs, and lobsters.

The fountain's designers, as if sensitive to Detroiters' ambivalence about Scott, placed his bronze image inconspicuously on the eastern edge of the terrace. The life-size figure of Scott is seated in formal attire on a throne-like chair, his lap now polished to gleaming gold by the thousands of children who have climbed onto it. Ironically, over the years, the figure of Scott has come to appear like a kindly patriarch.

C-11
Untitled
Stanley Dolega (b. 1942)
Belle Isle, Western End
1972
Painted steel

Perhaps the most difficult sculpture on Belle Isle for the general public to understand is this work by former Detroiter Stanley Dolega, who now lives in Wyoming. The piece consists of two bright blue rectangles—originally painted steel gray—whose exterior edges are rounded and interior edges are square. They are separated by a two-foot gap creating a definite, almost magnetic tension. While it can be appreciated as pure volume occupying space, the sculpture was meant to be an evocation of industrial forms, such as the stocky cement silos once visible, until their recent demolition, across the river on the Detroit skyline. As Dolega, who studied at Michigan State University and Wayne State University, put it, the work is "a composite of my experiences in Detroit."

Curiously, the sculpture also resembles a pair of statueless pedestals, forms that one finds in several traditional Belle Isle monuments. A smaller-scale piece by the artist, also comprised of identical halves, may be seen at Elmwood Park Plaza (see C-2).

C-12
Levi L. Barbour Memorial Fountain
Marshall Fredericks (1908–1998)
Belle Isle, Formal Garden West of Conservatory
1936
Bronze and granite

Levi Barbour (1840–1925) was a wealthy, civic-minded lawyer who led the fight to purchase Belle Isle for a city park. When he died, he left a generous bequest to beautify the island he loved. The inscription by Barbour on the rim of the outer basin pointedly suggests his civic motivations: "A continual hint to my fellow citizens to devote themselves to the benefit and pleasure of the public."

Marshall Fredericks, a young instructor of sculpture at Cranbrook (see A-24), won an open competition for a fountain design. The fountain is aligned with the Belle Isle Conservatory's central building, whose circular shape is repeated in the fountain's two stepped basins. A spirited bronze gazelle, its head thrown back, leaps exuberantly off a stylized rock at the fountain's apex. At the corners of the base of the pedestal Fredericks carved in black granite four animals native to Belle Isle—a rabbit, hawk, otter, and grouse— whose solid, chunky forms heighten our sense of the bounding movement of the bronze gazelle.

CUBA
PORTO RICO

ERECTED BY
THE PEOPLE OF
WAYNE COUNTY,
MICHIGAN
IN COMMEMORATION
OF THE SERVICE OF
HER VOLUNTEER SONS
IN THE ARMY, NAVY
AND MARINE CORPS
OF THE
UNITED STATES
DURING THE
WAR WITH SPAIN
1898 - 1902

C-13
**Spanish-American
War Monument**
Allen G. Newman
(1875–1940)
Belle Isle, Central Avenue
and Picnic Way
1932
Bronze and granite

This monument, with its symmetrical composition and centered stele, plaque, and inscriptions, pays tribute to the soldiers and sailors who served in the Spanish-American War of 1898. It also commemorates those who participated "during the Insurrection in the Philippines and the Chinese Relief Expedition—1889–1902." The ensemble's severe formality is softened by the relaxed poses and informal attire of the seven-foot-tall bronze soldier and sailor placed at either side.

The infantry man at left assumes the graceful pose of many a classical figure, with his left hip raised and his left shoulder lowered in a contrapposto position. With his hand in pocket, his cocked hat, open-collared shirt, and rifle cradled in one arm, he exudes confidence and quiet authority. His seafaring compatriot, who anchors the other side of the monument, stands barefoot on the sloping gunwale of a ship. He spreads his legs to maintain balance as the ship heaves; the wind seems to lift the collar of his shirt up the back of his neck and furl his wide-legged bell-bottom trousers around his ankles.

New York sculptor Allen G. Newman copyrighted this version of an infantry man in 1904 and over time produced more than twenty casts of the statue. Some are alternatively titled *The Hiker*, because of the long marches in military fatigues that foot soldiers in the Spanish-American conflict endured in a tropical climate. While created twenty-eight years later (in 1932), the sailor is remarkably similar in spirit and mood to Newman's earlier figure.

As a result of a recent restoration (1999–2000), the dark green patina of the two figures now contrasts strikingly with the gleaming white granite of the architectural support.

C-14
James J. Brady Memorial
Samuel Cashwan (1900–1988)
and Frederick C. O'Dell (1891–1979)
Belle Isle, Central Avenue,
between Picnic Way and
Inselruhe Avenue
1928
Bronze and granite

James J. Brady (1878–1925) founded the Old Newsboys Good-fellows of Detroit Fund in 1914. This unique philanthropic organization, made up of former newsboys, continues to sell papers each holiday season, the proceeds of which provide food, clothing, and toys for needy children throughout the City of Detroit. Sculptor Samuel Cashwan depicted Brady as he might have appeared on a windy street corner, a satchel over his shoulder and a paper for sale in his left hand. At his right side, shielded by his arm and overcoat, is a frail, barefoot girl, her hand grasping Brady's jacket. Architect Frederick C. O'Dell embraced the sculpture with a simple architectural pedestal and platform, whose horizontal and vertical lines sensitively echo those of the surrounding landscape. Born in Russia, Cashwan came to Detroit as a young boy and after study abroad taught sculpture at the College for Creative Studies and at the University of Michigan.

A later (1971) abstract hanging construction by Cashwan can be viewed from three levels in the lobby of the downtown Comerica Building (see A-29).

C-15
Major General Alpheus Starkey Williams
Henry Merwin Shrady (1871–1922)
Belle Isle, Central and
Inselruhe Avenues
1921
Bronze and granite

Detroit's first equestrian monument honors Alpheus Starkey Williams (1810–1878), who served with distinction in both the Mexican War (1846–1848) and the American Civil War. Commissioned in 1913, this imposing monument was not ready for dedication until 1921. New York sculptor Henry Merwin Shrady was a contemporary of Daniel Chester French (see A-8) and Augustus Saint-Gaudens, whose energetic equestrian monument of General Sherman (in Central Park, New York, 1900) is probably the best-known American example of this genre. Unlike Saint-Gaudens, Shrady chose to depict an unheroic moment in battle during a storm (to judge from the lowered head of horse and rider and the soldier's rain garb), when General Williams has paused to study a map of the battlefield. The horse's bowed head allows one's attention to focus on the vigorous silhouette of the general. In addition to his military career, Williams served Detroit as a lawyer, judge, publisher, postmaster, and congressman.

C-16
Johann Friedrich von Schiller

Herman Matzen (1861–1938)
Belle Isle, Central and
Vista Avenues
1907
Bronze and granite

Johann Friedrich von Schiller (1759–1805), a close friend of Goethe and an original and influential philosopher, advocated worldwide brotherhood and understanding. He expressed his passionate concern for personal liberty and human dignity in poems and dramas such as *Waldenstein* and *Wilhelm Tell*. His 1785 hymn to joy, "An die Freude," was used by Beethoven in the chorale finale to his *Ninth Symphony*. Unlike the Dante memorial across the street (C 17), with its intense, almost terrifying, portrayal of genius, the Schiller monument represents the German poet as a sensitive and compassionate individual who, index finger marking his place in a closed book, has paused to reflect on an idea. The monument is approached by a broad, low rise of steps, and the viewer is encouraged to move around the statue by the sideways direction of Schiller's gaze. Unfortunately the open space originally surrounding the sculpture has been circumscribed by the erection of a fence behind the figure. Inscribed on the sides of the pedestal are two quotations in German from Schiller's work. Danish-born sculptor Herman Matzen, who studied with Julius Melchers (see B-17) before moving to Cleveland, Ohio, in 1886, was commissioned by Detroit citizens of German descent to design the Schiller monument.

C-17
Dante Alighieri
Raffaello Romanelli (1856–1928)
Belle Isle, Central and Vista Avenues
1927
Marble

Dante (1265–1321) is considered the father of Italian literature. His *Divine Comedy* was the first major work written in Italian instead of Latin, the established literary language. In 1925, Italian sculptor Raffaello Romanelli was selected to create a statue commemorating the six hundredth anniversary of Dante's death. When funds for the pedestal were finally secured, the marble bust was erected on Belle Isle in 1927. The figure's costume, a high-necked cloak and hood crowned by a laurel wreath (a traditional symbol of honor), follows late medieval and Renaissance depictions of the writer. The emphatically frontal composition, stern expression, and staring eyes reinforce the sculptor's interpretation of the fierce dedication required of a great poet. The pronounced vertical axis that extends through the center of Dante's face and cloak is reiterated by the tall, narrow pedestal as well as by the use of marble for both figure and support.

C-18
Gazelle
Richard Bennett (b. 1954)
Belle Isle, Lakeside and Riverbank Drives
1991
Stainless steel

In the middle of a broad, grassy meadow near the water, Richard Bennett's tall, slim *Gazelle* rears dramatically twenty feet into the air. Its crisp, stylized silhouette distills the elegant form of a gazelle by focusing only on curved neck, angled head, and swept back, horizontal horns. The curving horns of this antelope become a single, streamlined shape that thrusts back and slightly upward in opposition to the forward lean of the arching neck. The daring, striking cantilever of the neck—the sole support of this slender but heavy sculpture—is braced by a steel armature underneath the gleaming, stainless steel cladding.

Bennett's interpretation of the agile grace of the gazelle stands in sharp contrast to a bronze gazelle by Marshall Fredericks, also on Belle Isle (see C-12), which, although somewhat stylized, is comparatively realistic and naturalistically detailed. A native Detroiter, Bennett envisions his Belle Isle *Gazelle* as the first of a proposed herd of five for the site. Other sculptures by the self-taught Bennett can be seen at the Charles H. Wright Museum of African American History in the Cultural Center (B-5) and at two locations in St. Clair Shores: *Waves* at Jefferson Avenue and Blossom Heath Boulevard and *Mermaid* at Harper Avenue and Twelve Mile Road.

C-19
Heidelberg Project
Tyree Guyton (b. 1955)
Heidelberg and Mt. Elliott Streets
1986–present
Mixed media

The unswerving social and artistic vision of Tyree Guyton has sustained the constantly evolving *Heidelberg Project* for more than twenty years. Born in Detroit, Guyton studied at the College for Creative Studies, Wayne County Community College, and Marygrove College. Founded by the artist with his grandfather Sam Mackey and former wife Karen Guyton in 1986, the block-long *Project* was initiated to reverse a blighted neighborhood's decline by transforming it into a streetscape of wonder and beauty. Guyton's imaginative recycling and display of city detritus, assembled with the assistance of friends, fellow artists, and an ever-present following of loyal neighborhood children, metamorphosed Heidelberg Street into a living, three-dimensional environment that garnered national attention.

Partially demolished in 1991 and 1999 by unsympathetic city administrations, the *Heidelberg Project* now exists as a reduced but still vibrant and kaleidoscopic artscape. Houses are embellished with both paint and objects, trees are festooned with handbags and trousers, and open areas are studded with suitcases, shoes, vacuum cleaners, tires, and doors. These salvaged goods, often found littering city streets, are revitalized in their new, densely packed surroundings. Vivid, multihued polka dots, a leitmotif unifying the disparate parts of *Heidelberg*, are painted over sidewalks and street, buildings, and automobiles. For Guyton, this ubiquitous and familiar image symbolizes an ideal state: harmony within diversity.

Another house, one block north, at Mt. Elliott and Elba streets, to which a menagerie of stuffed animals has been fastened, was added to the *Project* in 2005.

At once controversial, beloved, and reviled, Guyton's self-described "outdoor community museum" testifies to the potency of an artistic vision to transform both the spirit and physical appearance of a neighborhood. *Heidelberg Project* renewed a neighborhood through public engagement while creating a kind of rough-edged beauty from the discards of urban life.

To commemorate twenty years of the *Heidelberg Project*, a new outdoor sculpture by Guyton titled *Invisible Doors* was dedicated in the fall of 2007 in the outdoor courtyard of Wayne State University's Welcome Center at Warren and Woodward Avenues.

C-20
ABZ—Everything Is Anything
John Piet (b. 1946)
Pingree Park, East Warren Avenue at Seneca Street
1973
Painted steel

This vivid red construction has been described by its creator as a tripod about to move. It was part of sculptor John Piet's space series, in which he explored his interest in science fiction, creating pieces that seem to float in space. Situated near Pingree Park's northern entrance, *ABZ—Everything Is Anything* resembles the first letter of the alphabet and becomes a symbolic opening or gateway to this urban green space. The lithe and lyrical sculpture rises to a height of eighteen feet, crowned by a short, upward curving beam that lends a note of spontaneity and openness to the carefully contained construction below.

ABZ was restored and repainted in 1999. Other sculptures by Piet, who taught for many years at Macomb County Community College, are located in Harmonie and Chene parks (A-11, C-1).

C-21
Untitled
Arthur Schneider
(1926–1996)
Detroit Lions Academy
(formerly Julian H. Krolik
Elementary School), 10101
East Canfield Street at
Cadillac Boulevard
1962
Concrete

This engaging two-unit playscape by Detroiter Arthur Schneider is a witty personification of an interchange between a teacher and students. Commissioned by architect Louis G. Redstone for the entrance of a school he designed, the five-foot-tall, pebbled concrete duo has survived over forty-five years of the antics of clambering children. The teacher, formed of two open circles, one for the head and one for the torso, suggestive of a prehistoric idol, appears engaged in a dialogue or encounter with four children. Neatly aligned in a row, they become a single unit—as if joined at the hips—with equally sized ovoid-shaped heads. One youngster, however, is noticeably taller than the others.

Originally a low privet hedge enclosed part of the school's front lawn, creating a living fence and roomy courtyard around Schneider's sculpture that softened the angular lines of Redstone's building. The school's flat roof, exposed beams, low-slung profile, and freestanding covered walkways are of a piece with the unadorned organic abstract style of *Untitled*. Redstone was a forceful advocate of integrating art, whether two- or three-dimensional, in his buildings: schools, banks, and shopping malls, among others. He promoted his views through publications (see "Suggestions for Further Reading"), including works by Schneider here and elsewhere, along with commissions for Morris Brose, Samuel Cashwan, Mel Leiserowitz, and Robert Youngman.

Schneider, whose art is represented in numerous public venues in metropolitan Detroit, attended the University of Michigan and the Cranbrook Academy of Art. After a period of study with Italian sculptor Marino Marini, he exhibited widely in Europe and the United States during his lifetime.

C-22
Salute to Knowledge
Lyman Kipp (b. 1929)
Grosse Pointe Public Library,
10 Kercheval Avenue,
Grosse Pointe Farms
1981
Painted steel

Located on a broad, raised entrance podium in front of Marcel Breuer's austere Grosse Pointe Public Library, Lyman Kipp's red and blue *Salute to Knowledge* colorfully beckons to passersby. Fabricated of eight blue posts and five red, rectangular sheets of painted steel bolted together perpendicularly, the twenty-two-foot-tall *Salute* stands out boldly against the tawny brick of the library's façade. Like stiffened banners held aloft on slender poles, this simple, minimal piece "waves" and announces its spirited presence. Albeit abstract, the sculpture seems both to salute knowledge and to epitomize something of the lively, stimulating intellectual interaction one can encounter in a library. *Salute* was a gift from arts patron W. Hawkins Ferry, who also donated the Alexander Calder mobile that soundlessly circles high above the library's main reading room.

Born in New York, Kipp studied at both Pratt Institute (1950–52) and the Cranbrook Academy of Art (1952–54) before beginning a multifaceted career of teaching, exhibiting, and producing sculptural commissions.

C-23
Eastern Market Murals
Alexander Pollack (b. 1944)
Eastern Market, Russell and Winder Streets
1972
Wall paintings

The Eastern Market, Detroit's wholesale produce distribution center since the turn of the century, is also one of the few open-air farmers' markets still in operation in a large metropolitan area. By the early 1970s, the market façades were faded, peeling, and black with soot. Alexander Pollack, a young architect in the City Planning Department, was given the seemingly hopeless task of renovating the area. He turned the project into a virtual crusade and sold his ideas to forty shop owners. Vividly colored cornices and window caps, with murals illustrating what was sold inside, began to appear on buildings, and now bold, large-scale, cartoon-like characters enliven every available wall. Here, a trio of fruit-and-vegetable-laden baskets and crates are trundled to their destination over bumpy market streets. The market's success, particularly among Saturday shoppers, is due in part to Pollack.

C-24
Pope John Paul II
Ferenc Varga (1906–1989)
Pope Park, Joseph Campau Street at Belmont Street, Hamtramck
1982
Bronze and granite

Placed at the far end of Pope Park, the twelve-foot-tall figure of Pope John Paul II, mounted on a twenty-six-foot, two-story base, dominates the small, vest-pocket scale of this Hamtramck site. This sculpture, by Ferenc Varga (see also B-14), commemorates a 1969 visit to Hamtramck by Cardinal Karol Wojtyla of Poland. Varga's effigy of the pope, who appears to be blessing or preaching to multitudes from the top of a mountain or balcony, has been conceived in simple, rudimentary forms. The thick, heavy chasuble he wears is treated flatly: a basic rectangle with rounded corners, it is minimally detailed with an understated design that runs vertically down the front. Consequently, the pope's head and outstretched arms and hands create a dramatically stark silhouette against the sky.

The towering presence of this religious ruler of millions is humanized somewhat by a Dennis Orlowski mural (see C-25) adjacent to the statue, but at eye level, which captures the colorful street life and distinctive skyline of the city of Kraków where Wojtyla was once bishop.

C-25
History of Poland
Dennis Orlowski (b. 1944)
Holbrook Café, 3201 Holbrook Street, Hamtramck
1982
Acrylic on wood

Dennis Orlowski could be described as the muralist of Hamtramck, having painted a half dozen murals for interior and exterior locations in the city, were it not for the many other projects he has also completed in the metropolitan area over the last three decades. A lifelong resident of Hamtramck and a graduate of Wayne State University, Orlowski studied mural painting in Mexico City and New York. *History of Poland* is one of his largest compositions, stretching fifty-six feet (it is seven feet high) in two parts along the façade of the Holbrook Café. This restaurant occupies a site that was once the home of the Polish American Century Club, founded in 1917, which commissioned the mural. Orlowski recently restored and repainted the work.

In a bold, rhythmic style of alternating active and stately events and portraits, the *History of Poland* depicts key historical, religious, cultural, and political moments that shaped Polish society over the last one thousand years. The chronology begins at the far left with the introduction of Christianity to Poland in 966 and concludes at the far right with portraits of Pope John Paul II and Solidarity leader Lech Walesa. Intermittently between these two poles, the artist pictured the waxing and waning of the geographical map of Poland, as this frequently contested area changed rulers many times.

Other murals in Hamtramck by Orlowski can be seen at Pope Park (see C-24), at the Hamtramck Public Library, and at the H. Irving Mayson Neighborhood Center.

During the publication of this volume, the Holbrook Café closed and the murals removed from the outside of the building. They are scheduled to be relocated elsewhere.

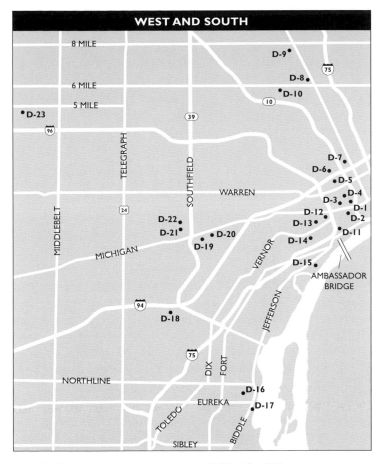

WEST AND SOUTH

8 MILE

6 MILE

5 MILE

D-23

TELEGRAPH

MIDDLEBELT

SOUTHFIELD

WARREN

MICHIGAN

VERNOR

JEFFERSON

DIX

FORT

TOLEDO

BIDDLE

NORTHLINE

EUREKA

SIBLEY

D-9

D-8

D-10

D-7

D-6

D-5

D-3 D-4

D-12 D-1

D-13 D-2

D-11

D-14

D-15

AMBASSADOR
BRIDGE

D-22

D-21

D-20

D-19

D-18

D-16

D-17

D-1. Mural
D-2. Father Clement Kern
D-3. Funnel Project
D-4. Untitled
D-5. Boy Scout
D-6. Martin Luther King Jr.
D-7. Geome-Tree
D-8. Ascension
D-9. Ernest W. Haass Memorial
D-10. Type "A" Personality
D-11. Penelopeia
D-12. Diversity Is Our Strength

D-13. The Corn Field
D-14. Clark Park Sculpture Project
D-15. Untitled
D-16. Count Casimir Pulaski
D-17. The Wyandots—A Family Tribute
D-18. Uniroyal Tire
D-19. Henry Ford
D-20. Untitled
D-21. Untitled
D-22. Untitled
D-23. Environmental Sculpture

D. West and South

D-1
Mural
Jerome Ferretti (b. 1952)
Michigan Avenue and Sixth Street
2005
Wall painting

The colorful wall painting by ceramic artist and painter Jerome Ferretti at the intersection of Michigan and Sixth marks the easternmost boundary of Corktown. The once predominantly Irish neighborhood, now known as "Detroit's oldest," dates from 1834. Ferretti's panorama shows an urban blend of gabled houses and downtown skyscrapers that are less than a mile away. The profiles of the Penobscot Building and GM World Headquarters, among others that tilt dynamically along opposing diagonals, are instantly recognizable.

Splayed across the foreground, on a representation of the still-extant red-brick pavers of Michigan Avenue, are three vehicles associated with neighborhood facilities and services: a yellow Checker cab, a U.S. Post Office delivery truck, and a bus that shuttles sports fans from parking and restaurants in Corktown to the baseball and football stadiums downtown. Bracketing this cartoon-like rendering of the urban scene are a purple light pole on the right and an animated red and yellow fire hydrant on the left that point to the zesty mix of this municipal area.

Ferretti, who studied at Wayne State University and the College for Creative Studies in Detroit, has fulfilled numerous commissions for both painted and ceramic installations in and of the city. Corktown's, sponsored by the Greater Corktown Development Corporation and a private donor, is one of his most recent. An earlier work (1998) consisting of an outsized pair of painted ceramic hands that represent the lower and upper peninsulas of Michigan is situated at the entrance to the Ford Underground Garage at Woodward and Jefferson avenues.

D-2
Father Clement Kern
Edward Chesney (b. 1922)
Trumbull and Bagley Streets
1985/1986
Bronze and granite

Father Clement Kern (1907–1983) was a charismatic, inspirational clergyman, as the inscription "Lift Up Your Hearts" on the pedestal of his monument attests. Assigned to a parish in the near-downtown area of Detroit (known as Corktown after its original Irish residents), Father Kern was a compassionate, generous cleric who worked tirelessly for the people of his neighborhood. In this life-size bronze by sculptor Edward Chesney, Kern leans forward, jacket unbuttoned, his arms open and gesturing, as if reaching out to a fellow individual or congregation. One hand, palm upward, moves toward the observer while the other cradles and displays a holy book. Bespectacled, with furrowed, lined brow, and by all reports a kind of "saint of the inner city," Kern exudes a warm and caring nature. Although his statue is locked within a gated and fenced enclosure for protection from vandals, Kern's generous, dynamic spirit nevertheless projects outward.

Native Detroiter Chesney studied with Ferenc Varga (see B-14) before embarking on a now well-established regional and national career as both artist and artisan, working not only in bronze but also in marble, wood, and fiberglass. An over-life-size bronze bust of Christopher Columbus by Chesney is located at Oakman Boulevard and Michigan Avenue in Dearborn.

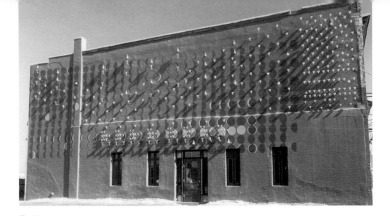

D-3
Funnel Project
Samantha Randall (b. 1969) with Gregory Holm (b. 1971)
and Abigail Newbold (b. 1976)
Slows Bar BQ Restaurant, 2138 Michigan Avenue at Fourteenth Street
2005
Paint, stainless steel, and aluminum

Funnel Project—cofunded by the Greater Corktown Development Corporation and Phillip Cooley, owner of Slows Bar BQ Restaurant—is an innovative hybrid of two-dimensional painting and three-dimensional installation. The striking piece is the work of Samantha Randall, a Cranbrook Academy of Art graduate who teaches architecture at the University of Texas–Austin, and collaborators Gregory Holm and Abigail Newbold.

Light and dark crescent shapes and glittery reflective funnels set against a sultry, reddish-purple background cover the two upper stories of a late nineteenth-century, three-story building. Interacting with changing light conditions, the funnels—some four hundred in differing sizes—create shadows that traverse the wall over the passing hours, producing a time-based, evolving visual experience rather than that of a single, fixed image. The phases of the moon, represented in horizontal rows, are based on a specific year, 1988, when the last train pulled out of the Michigan Central Station, the sad, no-longer-operating, and vandalized Beaux-Arts edifice (1913) across the street. Thus, a newly remodeled vintage building and its refurbished wall acknowledge an aging and imperiled structure that once serviced a city of nearly two million people. Michigan Central Station is a particularly poignant symbol of a mode of transportation that the Motor City has played such a major role in eviscerating.

Regrettably, the 2006 addition of a patio fence and shade trees next to the restaurant has partially obscured the lower register of *Funnel Project*.

D-4
Untitled
Graem Whyte (b. 1970)
Cochrane and Ash Streets
2006
Painted bronze, powder-coated
aluminum, and stainless steel

This untitled sculpture by Graem Whyte is one of six commissioned by the Greater Corktown Development Corporation for several vest-pocket-size parks in this North Corktown residential neighbor-

hood. The nonprofit community organization also funded the mural by Jerome Ferretti (D-1) situated along a nearby commercial strip.

Over the past two years, the construction of in-fill housing and restoration of extant homes have reinvigorated this formerly ravaged area. Both literally and figuratively, Whyte's proud and sturdy piece heralds this burgeoning development. Three cylindrical, stalk-like supports rise unimpeded some ten-and-one-half feet from the ground. Toward the top, they sprout complementary green and red growths, which in turn give birth to crimson-red buds. Whyte studied at Oakland Community College in Auburn Hills, Michigan, and the College for Creative Studies, where he serves as instructor and foundry technician.

A second sculpture, a carved stone fish by Tom Rudd, also enlivens this corner park. A totemic, stainless steel piece by Jason Huffines and a double-tower tribute to Rosa Parks and Martin Luther King Jr. by Alice Smith are located at other sites in the twenty-four-block district. Works by Taru Lahti and Jerome Ferretti will be installed in this section of Detroit in the near future.

135

D-5
Boy Scout
Robert Tait McKenzie
(1867–1938)
Boy Scouts of America Headquarters, Detroit Area Council,
1776 West Warren Avenue
1937 (cast 1965)
Bronze and concrete

Sculptor Robert Tait McKenzie, born in Canada of Scottish descent, was not only a well-known artist but also a practicing physician, lecturer in anatomy, and director of physical education at the University of Pennsylvania. McKenzie was an active supporter of the Boy Scouts organization, founded in 1908 by his friend Sir Robert Baden-Powell (1857–1941). Asked to produce a figure of an ideal scout for the Boy Scout headquarters in Philadelphia, McKenzie chose to portray the turning point from youth to manhood. The young scout, clutching his hat to his chest in a gesture of deference and firmly grasping his hatchet, seems to look confidently toward the future. The statue is one of eleven casts of the original work produced for various Boy Scout headquarters in the United States, Canada, and England.

Installed in front of the Detroit Boy Scout headquarters in 1965, the statue has since been moved indoors. Nevertheless, it is visible on the west side of the building in a projecting glass enclosure that recalls a reliquary containing a precious object.

D-6
Martin Luther King Jr.
Oscar Graves (1922–1990)
West Grand and Rosa Parks
Boulevards
1981
Aluminum

Partly hidden from casual pass-ersby, this commanding, three-foot-high head of Martin Luther King Jr. imposingly surmounts a four-foot-tall pedestal in a quiet, leafy, corner park. The Martin Luther King Jr. Memorial Park was designed and landscaped to lead the visitor up a shallow flight of steps to an outdoor viewing "room" or platform, creating a peaceful, semi-isolated oasis that actually fronts on a highly traf-ficked urban intersection.

King's visage, gazing straight ahead, was sculpted by Detroi-ter Oscar Graves, who studied at Wayne State University and the Cranbrook Academy of Art before working as an assistant to Marshall Fredericks (see A-24) for over a decade. Graves's likeness, three times life-size, is made of aluminum and portrays the charis-matic civil rights leader with a deeply thoughtful and perhaps mel-ancholy expression. Like the colossal head of some Egyptian noble or Roman emperor, that of King projects the formidable intellect of an impassioned leader. The steely gray patina of the sizable head, supported by a thick, sinewy neck, is made more powerful by its contrast with the light-hued concrete pedestal. Graves's bold and direct conception of King conveys the vivid presence of this leader both during and beyond his lifetime.

Graves also memorialized Richard Allen, the first bishop of the African Methodist Episcopal Church, in a bronze portrait medallion located in Nardin Park, Detroit.

D-7
Geome-Tree
Richard Bennett (b. 1954)
and Matt Corbin (b. 1945)
Clairmount Street and
Second Avenue
1987
Steel, concrete, stone,
and metal

In 1987, *Geome-Tree* be-
came the first art project
to be built on a city-owned
vacant lot. At the time, permission was given by the
City of Detroit Commu-
nity and Economic Devel-
opment Department as a
constructive use of an otherwise litter-strewn parcel of
land. Though the property has since reverted to private ownership,
the sculptural ensemble still stands more or less intact. As conceived
by Richard Bennett and Matt Corbin, the grouping included not
only the highly visible tower-obelisk-tree and a rotating arrow on
a tripod base, but also a sundial, circular well, two low-lying pyramids, and a set of steps flanked by two truncated "columns" (concrete sewer pipes set on end). The artists were assisted in both the
salvaging of discarded materials and *Geome-Tree*'s construction,
completed in just two weeks, by neighborhood and artist volunteers.

The centerpiece tower, thirty-five feet tall, is simultaneously
tree and Egyptian obelisk (it was formerly the boom of a crane).
The combination of Egyptian motifs (obelisk, pyramids, and two
Egyptian rulers shown in relief on the end of the kinetic arrow) with
industrial forms and materials is a tribute to the ethos of Egypt and
acknowledgment of the connection between ancient and modern
cultures. Moreover, the numerous geometric shapes—circles, triangles, trapezoids—suggest that geometry underpins both the practice
of art and the forms of nature.

Sculptor and teacher Corbin, who studied at the College for
Creative Studies, continues to oversee and maintain *Geome-Tree;*
sculptures by Bennett can also be seen at the Charles H. Wright Museum of African American History and on Belle Isle (B-5, C-18).

138

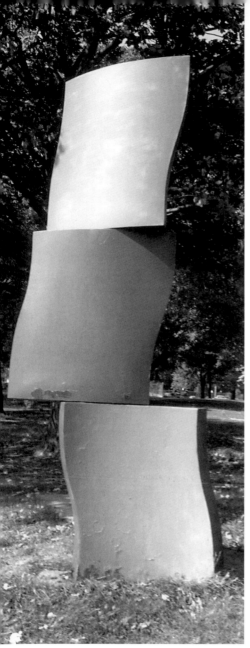

D-8
Ascension
Barry Lehr (b. 1951)
Palmer Park,
Merrill Plaisance Entrance
1977
Painted steel

This tall, slender, taxi-cab yellow construction by Barry Lehr rises like a beacon on a site just west of the main parking lot of Palmer Park. Born in New York, Lehr studied art at the University of Michigan and now lives in Philadelphia. His sculpture is composed of three curved, hollow steel slabs of the same basic shape, but turned, or rotated, and stacked at slightly different angles. The separate segments, mounted on a central shaft, were originally intended to pivot so that the wind or viewer could alter the work, but this idea was rejected because of its potential danger. The precarious balance of its components and its lively silhouette provide a contrast to the massive, low-lying *Merrill Fountain* on the east side of the parking lot. Selected by the Palmer Park Citizens Action Council and funded by the Department of Recreation of the City of Detroit, the sculpture was dedicated in August 1977.

D-9
Ernest W. Haass Memorial
Charles Keck (1875–1951)
Woodlawn Cemetery, 19975 Woodward Avenue
at West State Fair Avenue, Section 24
1927
Bronze and granite

This grave marker for Ernest W. Haass (1871–1925), Detroit physician and art patron, consists of a bronze bas-relief set into an arched, granite stele. Designed by New York sculptor Charles Keck, who studied with Augustus Saint-Gaudens (see A-8) from 1893 to 1898, the scene may refer to the little-known New Testament story of raising from the dead the twelve-year-old daughter of Jairus (Mark 5:22, Luke 8:41), although the girl in the relief would seem too old. The Christian belief in the eternity of the soul and existence of an afterlife is symbolized by the calm presence of Christ, in poignant contrast to the contorted posture of the distraught father carrying the pathetic, limp body of the girl.

Keck's emphasis on personal loss is mitigated as well by the verdant setting—the monument crests the top of a grassy slope against a backdrop of thriving trees—and its intimations of nature's cyclical process of renewal and regeneration.

D-10
Type "A" Personality
Mark Beltchenko (b. 1951)
Marygrove College,
8425 West McNichols Road
1995
Steel and paint

As befits its title, Mark Beltchenko's *Type "A" Personality* emerges assertively from the center of a two-tiered, circular garden, as if intentionally outstripping its flowering companions. The garden, named after Dr. Glenda D. Price, Marygrove College's president from 1998 to 2006, was her farewell gift to the school.

The steel sculpture appears to sway backward as it rises, like the flexible but strong stalk of a sturdy plant. While stem and blossom are apt descriptions of the piece's basic components, the title emphasizes the work's equally convincing likeness to a human body and head. The blossom/head comprises a three-sided square surrounding a tightly packed cluster of square and rectangular cubes; softly tinted with pale hues of ocher, rose, and silver, they temper the rigid steel and severe, rigorous geometry of *Type "A."* Set askew within their supporting grid, these blocky, hard-edged forms seem to be jostling among themselves for dominance and control, embodying the forces with which a competitive, driven personality must contend. Indeed, a tiny square poised precariously on the lower edge of the blossom/head of *Type "A"* may have been expelled for its weakness or imperfection. Marygrove's sculpture is one of three works by Beltchenko that evoke in an abstract language various patterns of human behavior. The other two—*Type "B" Personality* and *"Artist Type" Personality*—are similar to the college's piece in format and in height (approximately six-and-one-half feet).

Native Detroiter Beltchenko, who attended Alma College in Alma, Michigan, is also represented in the metropolitan area by installations at Detroit Zoological Park, Sterling Heights Civic Center, and the Boll Family YMCA in downtown Detroit.

141

D-11
Penelopeia
Caroline Blessing Browne Court (b. 1946)
United States Customs Inspection Facility, 2810 West Fort Street
1998–1999
Brick

Commissioned by the federal General Services Administration through its Art in Architecture Program, *Penelopeia*, by ceramist Caroline Blessing Browne Court, marks the entrance plaza of the U.S. Inspection Facility at the Ambassador Bridge. Detroiter Court, who studied art in Detroit (Wayne State University and College for Creative Studies) and in the East (Southeastern Massachusetts University), is known for brick sculptures that seem to defy gravity or, as here, require custom-made bricks to realize a particular form. The artist has also executed four carved, glazed brick murals for Beaumont Hospital (see F-5). Court, assisted by Robert Vandervennet, constructed *Penelopeia* on-site. The ten-foot-tall, red-brick arch rises from a diamond rather than a rectangular or square base. The sharp, crisp edge of the arch produced by the canted sides stands out clearly against the low, horizontally striped building.

Visible within the opening of the arch itself are almost three hundred uniquely carved bricks, whose images and names were inscribed by, among others, customs agents, architects, fellow artists, and high school students who were invited by the artist to collaborate in the genesis of *Penelopeia*. The interior thus discloses something personal and intimate, like a secret treasure, in contrast to its smoothly finished exterior.

The title alludes to the mythical weaver Penelope, Odysseus's wife in Homer's epic *The Odyssey*, whose dedication to her craft Court has admired and likened to her own commitment to art.

D-12
Diversity Is Our Strength
Los Galanes Restaurant, 3362 Bagley Street at Twenty-third Street, Rear Wall
1995
Wall painting

Designed by Arturo Cruz, an eighteen-year-old Nicaraguan who now lives in Canada, this gigantic mural was a collaborative effort involving at least seventy people. It was financed by several public and private grants and donors and supported by the owners of Los Galanes Restaurant, where it brightens the rear wall. The painters were multigenerational—ranging in age from four to sixty-seven—and multicultural. The concept for the painting originated at Freedom House, a Detroit-based shelter for political refugees and other ethnic people in need.

As the title emblazoned at the top proposes, Detroit's rich culture is one of its salient strengths. With hands outstretched to one another, Greeks, Italians, Africans, Indians, Arabs, Mexicans, and people of other nationalities line the roadway of the Ambassador Bridge, which connects Canada and the United States. Visible below the bridge are the skylines of Detroit and Windsor, as well as the flags of countries from all over the world, which also border the sides of the picture. At the bottom is a richly patterned, tapestry-like "landscape" teeming with flora and fauna. Covering two stories of a fifty-foot-wide wall, this vivid celebration of human diversity underscores, both literally and figuratively, a lofty vision of the harmonious interdependence of all peoples.

D-13
The Corn Field
Vito Valdez (b. 1952) and Jim Puntigam (b. 1952)
Bagley and Ste. Anne Streets
1997–1998
Wall painting

This arresting mural by Vito Valdez and Jim Puntigam on the side of a tortilla factory warehouse in Mexicantown testifies to the vital wall-painting tradition that flourishes in this ethnic enclave of Detroit. Valdez, an art instructor in the Education Department of the Detroit Institute of Arts, studied at the College for Creative Studies before embarking on a life and career devoted to community activism and environmental improvement. Other public murals by him are located at the Cobo Center Garage and at the Campbell Branch of the Detroit Public Library. In addition, *Big Fish*, a mixed-media sculpture representing "the Spirit of the Great Lakes," according to the artist, seems about to leap from a manmade hillock next to the I-375 Expressway, which cuts through Mexicantown.

Here, on Bagley Street, ably assisted by Puntigam, Valdez conceived *The Corn Field* as a deeply recessive landscape rendered in a complementary palette of golden yellow (day) and misty violet (night). Into the field (succinctly indicated by three retreating rows of corn in the center) file two lines, one of men, the other of women. Moving with great sobriety in rhythmic fashion, they participate in a never-ending going to and from the corn field, with the men harvesting during the day and the women returning to the village at daybreak to grind the corn to make tortillas for their families. They are separated from the viewers not only by the fact that their backs are turned to us but also by a trompe l'oeil, low stone wall that spans the bottom of the mural. Thus, they perform their elemental work, like a sacred ceremony in an otherworldly realm.

Tall text panels on either side of the vista of field and mountains (inspired by the landscape of El Paso, Texas) abruptly introduce present-day realities: on the right is the requisite list of funding sources that made the mural possible; on the left, the painting is dedicated to "the spirit of the indigenous people who cultivated the land that was once theirs."

The Corn Field, for all its utter simplicity—bilateral composition, two-color palette, precise one-point perspective, primal subject and setting—addresses issues that are not easily resolved. The loss of age-old patterns of living, the forfeiture of homelands, and the necessity to negotiate a fine line between acquiescence and resistance when adapting to a new culture are some of the affecting and bedeviling concerns brought forward here.

D-14
Clark Park Sculpture Project
Lila Kadaj (b. 1952) and students from
William C. Maybury Elementary School;
Michael McGillis (b. 1966) and students
from Western International High School;
Hector Perez (b. 1957) and students from
Amelia Earhart Middle School; Steven Rost
(b. 1953) and students from Western
International High School
Clark Park, Scotten Street between
Bagley and Porter Streets
1996–1998
Steel, bronze, brick, tile, and concrete

Four artist-teachers, in collaboration
with art students from the three schools
that overlook Clark Park on the city's
southwest side, produced this quartet of
artworks. Developed and executed over
the course of two years, this innovative
project was funded by many Detroit-area
groups, both public and private, including, among others, the Michigan Council
for Arts and Cultural Affairs, ArtServe
Michigan, the Department of Recreation
of the City of Detroit, Detroit Public
Schools, Barton Marlow Company, Outdoor Systems, and Disenos Ornamental
Iron.

While not thematically related, the
Clark Park project's components are
positioned within approximately twenty-
five feet of one another to form a loose
confederation. Composed of two slim,
totemic pylons (by Rost et al.), a basin
with peace symbol (by Perez et al.), a
decorative tile composition (by Kadaj et
al.), and a brick-and-steel seating unit
(by McGillis et al.), the several works
embody a spectrum of themes as well as
materials.

147

Release (Rost et al.) (*previous and this page*) furnishes visibility and a gateway, along with a sense of rising movement released into the sky through the spiky forms visible at the pylons' apexes. *A Wish for Peace* (Perez et al.) (*opposite top*) offers the peace symbol, roses clasped between a child's hands, and metaphorical nourishment via its deep basin. *People around the Universe: Our Green Land and Blue Water* (Kadaj et al.) (*not pictured*) presents a trio of tile patterns placed like a colorful surprise embedded in the grass. *Expanding Passage* (McGillis et al.) (*opposite bottom*) proffers seating for reflection as well as a passageway of progressively larger steel arches to transport one into another reality.

Sited under a shady canopy of mature trees, this gathering of art and ideas—and, by implication, the many who collaborated on it—is a salute to the spirit of cooperation, art-making, and ambitious striving. As Gere Baskin, the project's director, affirms, "The project offered the optimum opportunity for students and artists to plan, design, and build together—that in the end yielded not one, but an inviting cluster of sculptures created for both their community and Detroit."

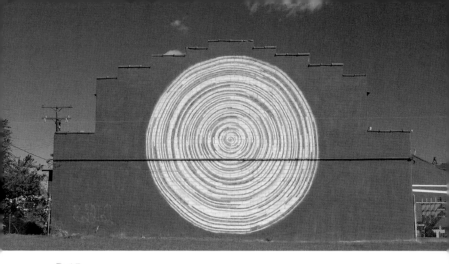

D-15
Untitled
Robert Sestok (b. 1946)
Edward W. Duffy and Company, 5840 West Jefferson Avenue, West Wall
1975
Wall painting

Robert Sestok's striking target was part of a unique experiment undertaken by industrialist and avant-garde art collector James F. Duffy Jr., who commissioned several young Detroit artists to make works of art for the interior and exterior of his pipe warehouse. Although Duffy no longer owns the company or the building, and the art formerly inside has been presented to Wayne State University, Sestok's mural remains on the warehouse wall. The painting, thirty-one feet in diameter, reflects in its shape and colors the industrial neighborhood of warehouses, loading docks, railroad tracks, and factories near the Detroit River and Ambassador Bridge. Made up of concentric circles and arc-shaped segments colored in various dull reds, greens, and creams, the target-like shape suggests a madly spinning saw or grinder, as well as the open end of a pipe. A recent repainting of the building in chocolate brown dramatically frames and showcases Sestok's kinetic image. Its somber palette and energetic centrifugal movement evoke the character of industrial Detroit and link Sestok with such contemporaries as James Chatelain, Michael Luchs, and Gordon Newton, who explored similar subjects. Also a sculptor, Sestok, who studied at the College for Creative Studies and Cranbrook Academy of Art, created *Continuity Tower*, which stands in the New Center area (B-29), *Dancing Hands* (A-14), and the *Laura Sies Memorial* (F-13).

D-16
Count Casimir Pulaski
Xaver Dunikowski (1876–1964)
Pulaski Park, Twelfth Street between Mollno
and Mulberry Avenues, Wyandotte
1936 (replica cast 1991)
Bronze and granite

This memorial to Count Casimir Pulaski, Polish patriot and American Revolutionary War general, was, according to the plaque affixed to its base, "erected by the citizens of Polish extraction of the city of Wyandotte, Michigan, to honor and perpetuate the memory of Brigadier General Casimir Pulaski." After participating in an unsuccessful revolt of Polish forces against the Russian-aligned king of Poland, Pulaski (1747/48–1779) came to America in 1777 to aid the colonists in their battle against the British. After he distinguished himself at the battle of Brandywine, he was made brigadier general in charge of cavalry by the Continental Congress and subsequently fought at Charleston, South Carolina, and Savannah, Georgia, where he was fatally wounded in October 1779.

In this bronze replica (fabricated in Detroit in 1991) of a deteriorating 1936 concrete original by Xaver Dunikowski, the nine-foot-tall figure of Pulaski surmounts a four-foot-high granite base. Dramatically posed in profile, Pulaski's aggressive stance and steely gaze are the embodiment of an active, vigorous military hero. Elbow and knees jut forward, boot-shod feet project beyond the base of the sculpture, and Pulaski raises his sword in defiance of the enemy before him. Behind, a flag curls around the general's body, emphasizing by its contrasting, curvilinear contours the sharp, forward momentum of this crusader for liberty.

Exhibited at the New York World's Fair in 1939, the statue arrived in Wyandotte in 1942 and was placed on a granite base that had been erected in 1938. Another monument to Pulaski, sculpted by Ferenc Varga (see B-14, C-24) in 1965, stands on Washington Boulevard in downtown Detroit.

D-17
The Wyandots—A Family Tribute
Michaele Duffy Kramer (b. 1947)
BASF Waterfront Park, 3625 Biddle Avenue,
Wyandotte
2000
Bronze

Elevated by a grassy knoll, a foot-high granite base, and the rocky bronze escarpment on which its figures are poised, *The Wyandots— A Family Tribute* by Michaele Duffy Kramer establishes a strong focal point for this riverfront park. The quartet of bronze, over-life-size personages represents a typical Wyandot family, the Native American peoples who originally lived along the shores of Georgian Bay, Lakes Huron and Erie, and the Detroit River. Over time, as their territory was ravaged by wars and unscrupulous land deals, the Wyandot resettled in Kansas and Oklahoma. Some, the Wyandots of Anderdon, still live in the downriver area.

Sculptor Kramer traveled to Wyandot gatherings to research the history of their lives. She chose, as she says, "to portray them in a happy moment surrounded by the everyday elements that make up their world." Positioned at the apex of the pyramidal grouping, the tall, dignified mother faces her seated son, who offers her the stringer of fish he has caught. To her left, her husband tenderly lifts their infant daughter so she can feed the shy, approaching fawn. The ensemble, intended to be viewed from the front, rests on a granite base on which is etched the images of all the principal plants essential to Wyandot survival—corn, beans, and squash—along with tobacco, sage, sweet grass, and cedar, which are sacred to their culture.

At the dedication of the piece, a millennial gift to the city's citizens from the Wyandotte Street Art Fair organization, three Wyandot chiefs, from Michigan, Kansas, and Oklahoma, professed their admiration for this sculptural tribute. A few years later, in 2004, the community-minded Street Art Fair Association commissioned a second bronze for the park. Its subject, a gathering of early settlers, created by John Nick Pappas (A-15), echoes the hierarchical configuration of Kramer's earlier work with the elder generation above and the younger below.

Kramer, who lives and works in Port Huron, Michigan, studied at the University of Michigan and in Florence, Italy, before serving an apprenticeship with Ferenc Varga (see B-14, C-24), from whom her realism in part derives. She is the author of an essay on the sculptural process of Marshall Fredericks (see A-24), who was a revered mentor to her in her artistic development.

D-18
Uniroyal Tire
Interstate Highway 94, Allen Park, South Side
1966 (refurbished 2003)
Rubber, steel, and paint

Refurbished in 2003 with paint, lighting, reflective and updated graphics, and Uniroyal's Web site address, the looming, eighty-foot *Big Tire* (as it is locally and familiarly referred to) is one of Detroit's best-known landmarks. For many traveling on I-94 to the city from the west, in particular from Detroit's international Metropolitan Airport, it is the first highly visible image one encounters. Originally designed as a tire-shaped Ferris wheel for the 1964–65 World's Fair in New York, *Uniroyal Tire* was transported by rail to Detroit and mounted on its concrete base on the south side of I-94 in 1966. Conceived and installed during the height of the Pop Art movement of the 1960s, the *Tire*, like the art and imagery of Roy Lichtenstein, Claes Oldenburg, and Andy Warhol, represents the ubiquitous, mass-produced goods for which the United States is recognized worldwide. The restored and modernized *Tire* promises to continue serving as a symbol of the Motor City's manufacturing prowess well into the future.

A colossal monument also indicative of Detroit's industrial identity is the house-sized "World's Largest Stove"; first shown at the 1893 World's Columbian Exposition in Chicago, it is on display at the Michigan State Fairgrounds at Woodward Avenue and Eight Mile Road.

155

D-19
Henry Ford
Marshall Fredericks (1908–1998)
Henry Ford Centennial Library, 16301 Michigan Avenue, Dearborn
1975
Bronze and marble

Henry Ford (1863–1947), who "put the world on wheels," is presented here by Detroit sculptor Marshall Fredericks (see also A-24, A-27, C-12, F-3, F-21) in a thoughtful pose. Dressed in a suit and tie, hands jammed in his pockets, and head inclined downward, Ford dominates this bronze and marble ensemble. In a formal, symmetrical composition, the auto magnate is flanked by four diamond-shaped, bronze reliefs that portray several scenes from his life: his school days, the four-square house he built, various Ford Motor Company buildings and products, and, significantly, Ford driving the Model T with the horse his invention dislodged relegated far into the background.

Fredericks designed the wide marble base and backdrop screen to add architectural substance to his monument, located at the far right corner of the dazzling, white marble façade of the Centennial Library. The dark green, heavily veined, antique marble selected by the sculptor not only adds weight but also establishes a dark foil for the lighter green surfaces of the life-size cast of Ford and the illustrative reliefs.

D-20
Untitled
Russell Thayer (b. 1934)
Ford Community and
Performing Arts Center,
15801 Michigan Avenue,
Dearborn
2001
Aluminum

To many Dearborn residents, the 2001 opening of the Ford Community and Performing Arts Center marked the city's cultural coming-of-age. Here, in a spacious, up-to-date facility, the performing and visual arts will be showcased well into the new century.

To celebrate this auspicious beginning, Russell Thayer proposed a freestanding portal for the circular drive entrance to the center. Like the passage of a visitor through the building's glass doors, Thayer's iconic gate offers a symbolic transition from one realm or state of mind to another. Drawing on the artist's familiarity with Asian prototypes, the untitled entranceway calls to mind the Torii gates of Japan whose symbolic function elicits comparisons to the carved gates of Indian stupas or the elaborate entrances to the castles and cathedrals of Europe.

Dearborn's twelve-foot-tall post and lintel gate is constructed of one-half-inch-thick cut aluminum plates supported by thin, graceful, wavy buttresses attached to their bases with highly visible nuts and bolts (a nod to the city's concentration of large manufacturing concerns). At its summit, a semicircular sun or moon portends a bright, promising future. Surrounded by lush plantings of tall grasses and a companionable bench (added in 2003), one can feel quite private and sheltered here despite its placement in a public setting.

Currently a lecturer at the University of Michigan, Thayer previously chaired the Art Department at Delta College in Bay City, Michigan, for many years. His educational background includes the University of Michigan; Royal College of Art, London; and Instituto Allende, San Miguel d'Allende, Mexico.

D-21
Untitled
Arman (Armand Fernandez)
(1928–2005)
Fairlane Town Center,
Southfield Expressway
and Michigan Avenue,
Dearborn, Court B
1976
Steel

Like other twentieth-cen-
tury sculptors, French artist Arman utilized ready-
made industrial materials,
but in his work they are
so transformed that their
former identity is lost. For
this piece in Fairlane Town
Center, the sculptor se-
lected a component culled
from the Detroit area—
truck grill guards—which
were donated by the Ford
Motor Company of Dear-
born, where the shopping
center is located. The rust-
colored units were assem-
bled and welded together at
the Fairlane site into a spiraling structure that rises
twenty-four feet, pulling
the eye up through the two-
story space. It is only near
the top that the recogniz-
able outline of the grill guard clearly emerges from the dense tangle
of metal below. This piece is part of a series called *Accumulations*,
in which the artist created sculptures not only with automotive parts
but also with such utilitarian objects as lightbulbs and paintbrushes.

D-22
Untitled
Chris Byars (b. 1939)
Fairlane Town Center,
Southfield Expressway
and Michigan Avenue,
Dearborn, Court A
1975
Painted steel

Coiling upward in a vast two-level space, this untitled work by Colorado sculptor Chris Byars fills its setting more aggressively than does Arman's skeletal, welded piece (D-21) in another area of the Fairlane shopping mall. Resembling an enormous, compact, coiled spring, Byars's structure rises to its full height of twenty-five feet in several tight reverse curves, in contrast to the sweeping, upward movement of Arman's construction. Byars's sculpture is constructed of quarter-inch steel plate, and its smooth surface is painted bright yellow. The work's curvilinear forms and enormous scale enable it to stand out clearly against the sharp, angular lines of the ceiling, balcony, and sunken conversation area of the hyperactive court.

D-23
Environmental Sculpture
Andrea Blum (b. 1950)
Livonia Civic Center, Farmington Road and Civic Center Drive
1992
Concrete, terrazzo, and steel

One approaches Andrea Blum's "invisible," below-ground-level work of art via a late twentieth-century version of a classical processional way, here gently inclined and bordered with plantings. The seventy-five-foot-long walkway leads to a broad esplanade that encircles a sunken enclosure. The enclosure is triangular, its wall made of concrete. A metal railing separates and safeguards the viewer from the area, which is about six feet deep. Accessed by two flanking staircases, the space is an open-air chamber to which one descends. It is "furnished" with a semicircular bench set on a low, stepped platform (also convex in shape), a low round table or seating unit, and a "carpet" of white gravel. Like a kiva, cella, or chapel that shuts out the distracting realities of quotidian life, Blum's *Environmental Sculpture* offers a quiet place for a restorative pause in the midst of the pell-mell cacophony of urban life. Indeed, the curves and angles of Blum's design respond to the shapes of the bustling, multistoried Livonia City Hall (1979) across the road. The building, however, rears up as assertively as the sculptor's sanctuary settles unobtrusively into the earth. As the artist cogently observes: "Once you got it [sculpture] off the pedestal . . . and then outside, sculpture was already on the road to becoming a whole different story."

New Yorker Blum, who is on the faculty of the Department of Art at Hunter College, New York, received degrees from the Boston Museum School of Art/Tufts University and the School of the Art Institute of Chicago. She has built permanent installations in the United States and abroad, including Boston, London, New York, Philadelphia, Den Hag, the Netherlands, and Strasbourg, France. A plaque near *Environmental Sculpture* credits the Livonia Cultural League for its leadership in securing the work and sensitively describes the salutary effect of experiencing the work: "The sculpture's lines draw our sprawling streets and subdivisions to our City Center and . . . provide the viewer the opportunity to become part of the environment of the sculpture. Its multi-levels simultaneously offer openness and enclosure. At the end of the day, like the city residents, it slips into the dark of the night." Unfortunately a bronze sculpture of geese in flight, which was placed to one side of Blum's plaza at a later date, disrupts the muted equilibrium of her original design.

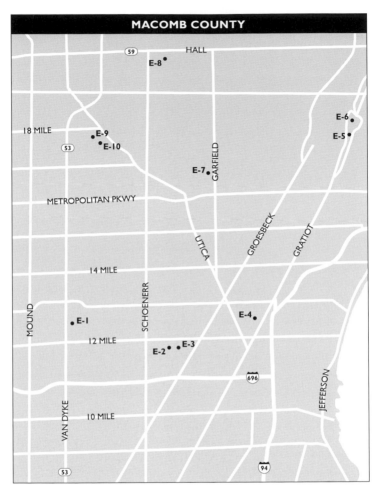

MACOMB COUNTY

E-1. Dawn
E-2. Crystal Transformation
E-3. Glacial
E-4. The Rosebuds
E-5. County Seat

E-6. Galileo's Night Vision
E-7. Martin Luther
E-8. Six-Tonner for Julian
E-9. The Spirit of Sterling Heights
E-10. Burst

E. Macomb County

E-1
Dawn
David Barr (b. 1939)
Warren Civic Center, 29500 Van Dyke Avenue, Warren
2006
Stainless steel and granite

The recently completed Warren Civic Center complex is distinguished by a sleek, glass-fronted city hall/library and a tall, slender, red-brick clock tower overlooking a spacious, two-acre plaza.

Reminiscent of a traditional town square, the plaza includes a broad, grassy sward and an oval reflecting pool/skating rink with centralized fountain. Both fountain and a towering portal titled *Dawn* were designed by David Barr who, born and raised in Detroit, was for many years a professor of art at nearby Macomb Community College.

The asymmetric portal, constructed of twenty stainless steel cylinders ranging in length from six to twenty-eight feet, forms a thirty-four-foot-high circular gateway to the suburb's civic hub. Like many such structures (see B-13, D-20, E-9), it represents a symbolic gateway to an official or ceremonial precinct. The adjacent fountain, twenty-four feet tall, is also formed of cylindrical units, but it is configured into an upwardly spiraling form that reads as a circle when viewed head-on. Notably, the curving forms of both structures are created by the welded clustering of perfectly straight, daringly balanced elements. Together, the wide portal of *Dawn* and tightly curled spiral of the fountain stand out strikingly against the crisp, right-angled design of freestanding clock tower and city hall. The vivacious contrast of architecture and sculpture signifies the lively juxtapositions of a civic concourse, as well as an older suburb's decision to relocate and update the basic components of a municipal center to signal a fresh vision for the twenty-first century.

Interestingly, when *Dawn* is viewed from city hall rather than in conjunction with the building, its carefully planned siting establishes as well a dynamic relationship between it and the rectilinear/modernist architecture of the 1950s-era General Motors Technical Center. Located directly across Van Dyke Road from the Civic Center, the GM buildings were designed by Eero Saarinen, best known perhaps for his design of the TWA terminal at Kennedy International Airport.

Barr, responsible as well for *Transcending* (A-23, codesigned with Sergio De Giusti) and *Crystal Transformation* (E-2), which are also based on circular schemes, suggests that "*Dawn* means a new age and revitalizing. . . . It's about expressing energy and a high-tech feeling of energy too."

E-2
Crystal Transformation
David Barr (b. 1939)
Macomb County Community College,
The Commons, South Campus
14500 Twelve Mile Road, Warren
1976
Painted steel

As highly geometric and nonobjective as David Barr's work appears to be, it is nevertheless inspired by underlying natural processes of growth, development, and change. The nine units of *Crystal Transformation,* ranging in size from two-by-two-by-four feet to four-by-four-by-eight feet, grow larger and change color (from brown to bright blue and then to pale blue) as they move in a broad arc from the bottom to the top of a small hill. The first and smallest component of the suite seems to emerge from the ground, the next units become progressively larger and more independent of the ground, and the last sections appear to collapse back into the earth. Thus, these forms, recalling atomic, cellular, crystalline, or organic systems, are a celebration of natural life and death cycles. Other works by Barr can be seen at the Fairlane Town Center, Dearborn; Chrysler Corporation, Auburn Hills; and at Oakland University in Rochester Hills.

In addition, an ongoing multi-unit sculptural project by Barr and participating communities, titled *Coasting the Base Line*, has been underway since 2003. This long-term, open-ended undertaking encompasses a series of ten-foot-tall obelisks situated along Michigan's Base Line (Eight Mile Road in some places), which runs from the coast of Lake St. Clair to the shore of Lake Michigan. Thus far four obelisks, constructed of alternating slabs of black and white granite to suggest a surveyor's pole, have been installed in Grosse Pointe/Harper Woods, Farmington/Farmington Hills, Northville, and Novi.

E-3
Glacial
Ivy Sky Rutzky (b. 1948)
Macomb County Community College, The Commons, South Campus,
14500 Twelve Mile Road, Warren
1977
Stainless steel

Ivy Sky Rutzky's audaciously simple sculpture, *Glacial*, consists of two quarter-inch stainless steel planes, one essentially rectangular (five by ten feet) and the other triangular (three feet per side). The steel sheets have been polished to a high sheen and laid flat into an expansive sloping lawn. Suggesting airborne views of glacial lakes, or pools of standing or frozen water, *Glacial*, which is sculptor Rutzky's first outdoor piece, expresses her reverence for natural and pure forms as well as her interest in creating out-of-door sculpture that does not intrude upon the natural setting. Alas, over the years the grass has overgrown the edges of the steel plates, noticeably reducing their visibility.

A graduate of Wayne State University, former Detroiter Rutzky now lives and works in New York.

E-4
The Rosebuds
Janet B. Trimpe (b. 1943)
Roseville City Hall, West of
29777 Gratiot Avenue and
South of Common Road at
VFW Memorial Drive
2001
Bronze

But for the fact that they are larger-than-life and cast in bronze with a brownish-gray patina, Janet B. Trimpe's sculptural group could be an actual middle-class family striding across the plaza leading to Roseville's city offices and library. The placement of a mother, father, and three children, all directly on the ground, enhances the palpable reality of the figures.

The five-member family, whose crisscrossing glances and mutually genial, smiling expressions exemplify an idealized compatibility, appear sufficient unto themselves. Mother and father turn toward each other, while the children gaze either at their parents or one another. The parents, informally garbed in casual tops (his a polo shirt, hers a V-neck) and slacks (jeans?), carry two of their offspring: one rides piggyback on his father while another is slung sidesaddle on her mother's hip. The third, in typically childlike behavior, toddles along, dragging his upside-down teddy bear behind him. *The Rosebuds*, the title, refers, according to the artist, to the children who, like flower buds, will soon blossom and impact the future of society at large.

Trimpe, who studied sculpture at the College for Creative Studies in the late 1970s, is a proficient portraitist—from a three-dimensional bronze of Mayor Orville Hubbard (1989) that commands a site in front of the Dearborn City Hall to a three-quarter bas relief effigy of John D. Dinan, the late Farmington city manager unveiled in 2007 on the grounds of the Farmington City Hall. However, she has focused her energies in the last several years on multifigural ensembles for city halls, parks, and other public places that can be found from Dearborn to Belle Isle to Mt. Clemens to Roseville.

E-5
County Seat
Gary Kulak (b. 1952)
Cass Avenue and South Walnut Street, Mt. Clemens
1999
Painted steel

Prior to 1999, only three representational monuments, one of General Alexander Macomb by Frank Varga (1977) (see B-14), a bust of John Fitzgerald Kennedy by Marshall Fredericks (1970) (see A-24), and a statue of St. Joan of Arc constituted the major examples of

public art in Mt. Clemens. But in August of that year the Mt. Clemens Art in Public Places program introduced its first acquisition, *County Seat* by Gary Kulak. Spearheaded by the Art Center (now the Anton Art Center), several additional works were installed in short order, rapidly swelling the complement of public art in the city.

Kulak's royal blue *County Seat*, nestled in foliage at a corner location, is a spare but metaphoric acknowledgment of the city's central importance to the county. Extending twenty-four feet into the air, its seat eight feet aboveground, the sculpture dwarfs one's usual expectations of "chairness." This signature image of the sculptor's oeuvre, one he has produced in a diverse range of materials, heights, and girths, suggests anthropomorphic associations as well: arms, legs, backs, and seats after all are integral components of chairs.

County Seat's slim, steel structure, which one can walk around as well as under, also functions as a framing device for the surrounding urbanscape, including the Art Deco Macomb County Building, which is visible from here. Though lacking an actual seated human, Kulak's chair calls to mind the many worthies, memorialized ensconced in sundry chairs, from simple to throne-like, in the metropolitan region (see A-6, A-7, C-10, C-16). In an era that values transparency in governance, *County Seat* seems tailor-made for the twenty-first century. As an added dividend, the sculptor, noting the attenuated scale of his piece, suggests that "it allows adults to be children again. It draws them back to a sense of purity."

Kulak, who hails from Pennsylvania, studied at the Cranbrook Academy of Art and at Hunter College, New York. He has been a longtime resident and practicing artist in southeastern Michigan.

Galileo's Night Vision
Joseph Wesner (1955–2002) and James Storm (b. 1970)
Main and Market Streets, Mt. Clemens
2002
Cor-ten and stainless steel

The sculptor Joseph Wesner, who played football and competed
as an oarsman, once observed that "The kinesthetic qualities of an
athlete can be found in my work." Approaching his *Galileo's Night
Vision*, it is hard to resist its visceral expression of perpetual rota-
tion. Are the several concentric, seemingly free-floating, thin steel
arcs about to spin off into the air, or might they instead be on the
verge of coalescing with the two shallow conical forms, five feet in
diameter, that dominate the sculpture?

Invoking Galileo (1564–1642) and his visionary theories in the
piece's title, Wesner allied the astronomer's intellectual energies
with athletic prowess. The eye-like coronas, one dark, rusty, and

absorptive, the other silvery, smooth, and reflective, appear to scan the skies like satellite dishes seeking signals and images. The shallow, stepped base grounds and stabilizes the sense of constant motion it supports.

A pivotal artist's residency in China in 1990 introduced Wesner to concepts and forms of China's age-old culture that overlap with Western beliefs. He discovered that a circle, with a central hole for passage to nirvana, is the Chinese symbol for heaven. Galileo's vision of the solar system and Buddhist transcendence are both cosmic visions. On a less spiritual level, the shallow cones the artist began to employ in works such as this recall the round, peaked hat, often called a "coolie," worn by Chinese laborers for millennia.

A native of Philadelphia, Wesner attended Georgetown University and the Cranbrook Academy of Art. Joining the faculty of the College for Creative Studies (CCS) in 1984, he served as professor and chair of the sculpture program until his untimely death in 2002. James Storm, his assistant, worked closely with the sculptor on the fabrication of *Galileo*. A related work by Wesner is installed in front of the entrance to the Anton Art Center, Mt. Clemens, and other works can be found on the campus of CCS in Detroit.

E-7
Martin Luther
Ernst F. A. Rietschel (1804–1861)
Cadillac Memorial Gardens-East,
38425 Garfield Road,
Clinton Township,
Northeast Quadrant/Section
1930
Bronze and granite

This imposing monument to Martin Luther measures twenty feet from the base of the granite pedestal to the crown of the head. It is one of six bronze replicas in the United States of a twice-life-size effigy of the religious leader that is part of a memorial in Worms, Germany, to the leaders of the Protestant Reformation by Ernst F. A. Rietschel (1861–1868). Luther was summoned to Worms, on the Rhine River, in 1521 by Emperor Charles V to retract his writings and recant his doctrines. In this medieval city he uttered his defiant declaration, excerpted on the statue's plaque, that became the rallying cry of Lutheranism: "Here I stand. I cannot do otherwise."

Wearing the capacious, loose-fitting robe of a doctor of theology, the revolutionary reformer seems to rap his clenched fist on the weighty Bible he holds and juts one boot-shod foot emphatically forward from the pedestal. He emphasizes the strength of his convictions by seeming to raise his head toward the higher power that fuels his beliefs. Framed by a tall semicircle of cedars, "the father of the Reformation" looms large as a stern but admirable man of courage and steadfastness.

To "signalize" (as per the plaque) the Quadricentennial of the Augsburg Confession in 1530, when Luther promulgated the fundamental principles of the Lutheran faith, the Luther Memorial Park Association selected, among the many portrayals of Luther, Rietschel's dramatic and vigorous characterization. The monument was dedicated in 1930.

E-8
Six-Tonner for Julian
Bruce Beasley (b. 1939)
Lakeside Shopping Mall,
14600 Hall Road,
Sterling Heights, West Court
1975–1976
Painted steel

Named for his son, this piece by California sculptor Bruce Beasley is one of five works commissioned for Lakeside Shopping Mall by the developer, the Taubman Company, Inc. Painted fire-engine red, the work resembles a giant origami paper construction. It is composed of interlocking hexagonal units that become increasingly complex in their arrangement as the sculpture climbs to a height of twenty-five feet. Analogous to the growth of a child, *Six Tonner for Julian* zigzags in opposing directions before coalescing to reach its lofty elevation. At the same time, Beasley successfully created a monumental form whose aggressive presence is equal to the vast scale and activity of the court in which it is sited.

E-9
The Spirit of Sterling Heights
Marcia Wood (1933–2000)
Sterling Heights Civic Center, City Hall, 40555 Utica Road
1990
Painted aluminum

Standing at the entrance to the Sterling Heights Civic Center, Marcia Wood's *Spirit of Sterling Heights* evokes an ancient Roman arch. Linking past and present, Wood's classical arch, sited in front of the suburb's 1960s city hall, also functions as a welcoming, symbolic portal to the complex of structures that make up the city's offices. Measuring a generous sixteen feet tall and an expansive nine feet wide, the embracing contour of the arch is given a decidedly modern edge through Wood's angular, serrated outline. Several cut, pierced, and joined vertical elements that fill part of the opening suggest a door ajar, as if inviting all passersby to walk through. Fabricated of painted aluminum, *The Spirit*'s silvery, vertically striated patina displays a surface sheen accentuating the piece's simple, silhouetted shapes. Muted in color, the sculpture is less assertive than

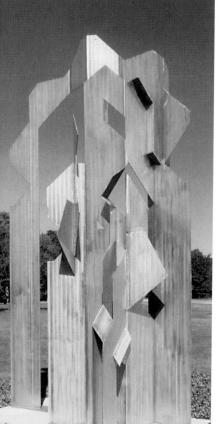

if it had been painted the bold red hue originally proposed by the sculptor.

Michiganian Wood studied at the Cranbrook Academy of Art and Kalamazoo College, Michigan. Her sculptural oeuvre is additionally represented in the metropolitan area by a twelve-foot-high, stainless steel cluster of wavy forms, titled *Standing Together* (1980), on Washington Boulevard and Clifford Street in downtown Detroit. Its subject of unity in diversity is related to but quite differently realized than that of *The Spirit of Sterling Heights*.

E-10
Burst
Ray Katz (b. 1938)
Sterling Heights Civic Center, Utica and Dodge Park Roads
2003
Aluminum

Burst, an eleven-foot-tall, welded-aluminum assemblage by Ray Katz, was recently acquired (2006) by the city of Sterling Heights and serves as a spirited companion to Marcia Wood's *Spirit of Sterling Heights* of 1990 (see E-9). Her inviting, expectant gateway and his exuberant cluster of geometric elements capture the promise and energy of this suburban enclave. Katz's composition literally "bursts" open at its apex. A sturdy, splayed tripod of two square beams and a cylindrical pole lean inward and upward, piercing two constricting forms—a circle and a square—as they extend into space. The resulting visceral sense of ecstatic release captures the processes of change that one can undergo in the course of a lifetime. Indeed, the piece was purchased for the civic center grounds in large part because during its "temporary" two-year-long installation on the site, it had received enthusiastic and positive reactions from city residents.

Katz's creative practice of composing spontaneously before finalizing his design is apparent in *Burst.* Its completed configuration, perhaps calling to mind a handful of pick-up sticks before they are let go, is extemporaneous in feeling. Though its welded fabrication in the end fixes all the components securely in place, the element of chance that plays a significant role in the sculptor's procedure remains prominent.

Katz grew up in Detroit and studied at the College for Creative Studies, Eastern Michigan University, and Wayne State University. He teaches art at Oakland Community College in Auburn Hills and maintains a studio in Pontiac, where he builds his large-scale outdoor works. Another sculpture by the artist is installed in Detroit's Chene Park (see C-1).

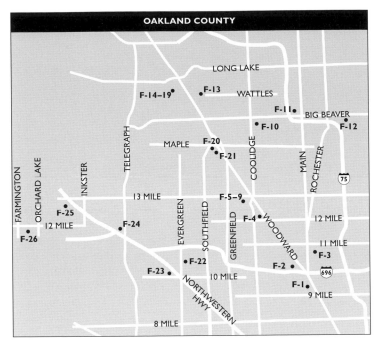

OAKLAND COUNTY

LONG LAKE

F-13

F-14-19 WATTLES

F-11

BIG BEAVER

F-10 F-12

TELEGRAPH

MAPLE F-20

F-21

COOLIDGE

MAIN

ROCHESTER

75

13 MILE F-5-9

FARMINGTON

ORCHARD LAKE

INKSTER

EVERGREEN

SOUTHFIELD

GREENFIELD

F-4

WOODWARD

12 MILE

F-25

F-24

12 MILE

F-26

11 MILE

F-3

F-22 F-2

F-23 10 MILE

NORTHWESTERN HWY

F-1

9 MILE

696

8 MILE

F-1. Billboard
F-2. Horace H. Rackham Memorial Fountain
F-3. Star Dream
F-4. Spirit of the American Doughboy
F-5. Ribbon Fall
F-6. Michigan Garden
F-7. The Echo of Flora Exotica
F-8. Progression
F-9. Celestial Walk
F-10. Sticker Woman
F-11. Reflective Head
F-12. Blue Chip
F-13. Laura Sies Memorial

F-14. Sunglitter
F-15. Europa and the Bull
F-16. Jonah and the Whale
F-17. Orpheus Fountain
F-18. Cranbrook Ingathering
F-19. For Mother Teresa
F-20. Upcast
F-21. The Freedom of the Human Spirit
F-22. City of Southfield
F-23. Drifter
F-24. Stargazer (for Columbus Cain)
F-25. Covington
F-26. Humoresque

F. Oakland County

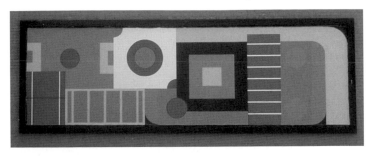

F-1
Billboard
Various artists
Woodward Avenue at West Maplehurst Street, Ferndale
1993–present

The eight-by-twenty-three-foot *Billboard*, mounted on the north wall of the building at Woodward and Maplehurst, has served as a short-term exhibition space for numerous artists since 1993. Unlike a standard billboard display or wall painting, whose advertisement or imagery is on view for long periods of time (often many years in the case of wall paintings), this public forum changes approximately every eight weeks, which permits as many as six or seven different designs per year. Since each project is intended to be temporary, the artist-designers are liberated from the usual concerns about durabil-

ity and permanence but must consider scale, readability, and their municipal audience.

Over the fourteen-year history of the *Billboard*, artists as diverse as Hartmut Austen, Phaedra Robinson, Nick Sousanis, and the collaborative Object Orange, among many others, have conceived and executed a broad spectrum of two- and three-dimensional works for the wall. Object Orange (*bottom*) attached a collection of urban detritus, the whole painted construction-barrel orange, in a freeform composition, while Nick Sousanis (*opposite bottom; this page, top*) affixed vertical flanges to his scheme so that the imagery flipped from shuffling sleepwalkers to leaping dancer as drivers sped by. For their part, Austen (*opposite top*) and Robinson (*opposite center*) designed large-scale compositions for the space, the former a bright and athletic interplay of colored shapes, the latter a brushy, flickering white form overspreading a sultry red background.

Originally sponsored by Revolution, a gallery formerly housed in an adjacent building, and then by the Lemberg Gallery, a few doors south on Woodward, it is now funded by the Public Art Project, a Michigan nonprofit, and coordinated by the staff of the Lemberg Gallery. Whether privately or publicly supported, this accessible, ongoing panorama of artworks is always fresh, often provocative, and never the same twice.

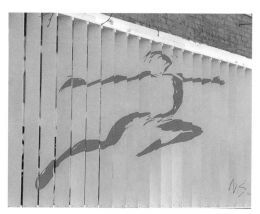

F-2
Horace H. Rackham
Memorial Fountain
Corrado Joseph Parducci (1900–1981) and Frederick A. Schnaple (1872–1948)
Detroit Zoological Park, 8450 West Ten Mile Road, Royal Oak
1939
Bronze and granite

Opened in 1928, the Detroit Zoological Park was one of the first zoos to display animals in barless enclosures simulating their natural habitats. Horace H. Rackham (1858–1933) was long involved with the zoo and served as first president of the Zoological Commission from 1924 to 1928. His widow, Mary Rackham, presented the fountain and reflecting pool to the zoo. Dominating the expansive pool lined with blue tile are two playful ten-foot bronze bears sharing the base with several life-size turtles and frogs. Flanking this central group are two subsidiary fountains composed of sleek, graceful seals perched on rocks. Sculptor Corrado Joseph Parducci, known for his many architectural reliefs around Detroit, and designer Frederick A. Schnaple created an impressive and popular focal point for the zoo's central mall.

Works by a number of other artists—David Barr (E-1), Marshall Fredericks (A-24), Inuk Charlie, Gretchen Kramp, Jim Pallas, and Mary Chase Perry Stratton—can also be found in the buildings and on the grounds of the zoo. In fact, the establishment of the Richard and Jane Manoogian Endowment for Wildlife Art and Interpretation in 2001 ensured that the zoo would be able to maintain its fine art collection and acquire new works for display.

F-3
Star Dream
Marshall Fredericks (1908–1998)
City Hall, Barbara Hallman Plaza,
Williams and East Second Streets,
Royal Oak
1997
Bronze, stainless steel, and granite

This soaring ensemble by nationally known artist Marshall Fredericks, who created numerous sculptures in the metropolitan area (see A-24, A-27, C-12, D-19, F-21), towers forty feet above a landscaped plaza between the library and city hall of Royal Oak. Formally approached by walking down an eighty-foot alley of young trees, the two thirty-foot-tall, green patinated nudes appear to be slowly ascending. Contributing to the sense of levitation is the off-center placement of the female figure, who seems to rise into the sky unsupported, purely of her own volition.

Titled *Star Dream*, both figures are indeed serene and ethereal, their hair swept back and eyes closed, as if in silent communion with a lofty vision to which they aspire. His arms, spread wide in quiet jubilation, seem to reach toward some intangible "dream," while hers fall relaxed at her side. Only the slight turn of the woman's head mitigates the formality and frontality of Fredericks's design.

The emblem of the star itself is introduced in the ten-foot-high cluster of three-dimensional, stainless steel stars that form the highly reflective base for the duo. Ascending side by side, separate but together, the male and female figures of *Star Dream* embody a city's idealized view of its citizens' pursuit of their dreams.

F-4
Spirit of the American Doughboy
Ernest M. Visquesney (1876–1946)
Roseland Park Cemetery, Woodward Avenue
and West Twelve Mile Road, Berkley, Southwest Quadrant
1920/1934
Bronze and granite

In 1920 Ernest Visquesney realized his objective to create, as he put it, "the only absolutely perfectly equipped and historically correct example of what the United States infantry soldier was, and stood for." Described on its base as *Spirit of the American Doughboy*, the term, whose nineteenth-century origins are still subject to speculation, became the universally popular nickname for American troops sent to Europe to fight in World War I. In the two decades following the armistice in 1918, numerous monuments were raised to remember the soldiers who fought in "the war to end all wars," and in many of them Visquesney's statue was the centerpiece. It was first copyrighted in 1922, then slightly modified and recopyrighted in 1934; well over one hundred replicas are thought to exist in more than twenty-five states.

Roseland Park Cemetery's memorial is an example of the 1934 *Doughboy*. Heading into battle, the infantryman strides purposefully across a no-man's-land whose barrenness is indicated by two blasted tree stumps fore and aft. The soldier opens his mouth in a shout; the hand of his upraised right arm clutches a grenade while his left hand grasps a bayoneted rifle. (The bayonet, alas, has been broken off.) He is well equipped: he carries a bedroll backpack over his shoulders, a gas mask pouch on his chest, and a cartridge belt and canteen at his waist. The determined soldier is shown as he heads into battle: his unhesitating, forward momentum and battle cry convey his courage and the moral rightness of the U.S. cause more effectively than had the sculptor chosen to represent a melodramatic scene of victory or a poignant death in combat. Now all but overshadowed by a grove of evergreens, the seven-foot-high figure, mounted on an equally tall, tapering granite pedestal, was erected by the Wayne County Council Veterans of Foreign Wars and dedicated in 1941.

Visquesney, an Indiana native and son and grandson of French sculptors, spent seventeen years working for monument makers in Georgia. In 1922 he resettled in his home state to manage his expanding sculptural practice.

F-5
Ribbon Fall
Glen Michaels (b. 1927)
William Beaumont Hospital, 3601 West Thirteen Mile Road,
Royal Oak, Main Entrance, East Tower
1996
Fused colored glass

The ravishing spectrum of color and luminosity of *Ribbon Fall* by
Glen Michaels is a result of the artist's mastery of the technique
and properties of working with fused colored glass. Here the effect, according to the artist, "is reminiscent of a child's paint set
spilling into the pool." The flowing rivulets of color, set against a
black glass background, stream down the eight-by-fourteen-foot
wall and puddle at its base. Planted with shrubs, trees, and flowers,
this edenic space, known as Employees Park, provides a lush oasis
within an institutional selling.

A Troy resident, artist Michaels, born in Spokane, Washington,
studied at the Cranbrook Academy of Art (where he later taught),
at Wayne State University, and at the University of Windsor. He is
represented by numerous commissions in the Detroit area, including, among others, large-scale wall relief sculptures of mixed media
at the Henry Ford Centennial Library, Detroit Receiving Hospital
(see B-4), Henry Ford Wyandotte Hospital, and the Mt. Clemens
Public Library.

Michaels's *Ribbon Fall* is just one of a number of artworks in various media in the evolving Beaumont Collection that also includes
examples by Michelle Andonian, Dirk Bakker, Caroline Blessing
Browne Court (see D-11), Joyce Cram, Gerome Kamrowski (A-
36f), Jun Kaneko, Harold Linton, Steven Magsig, Gene Meadows,
George Vihos, and Larry Zox.

186

F-6
Michigan Garden
Mollie Fletcher (b. 1951)
William Beaumont Hospital, 3601 West Thirteen Mile Road,
Royal Oak, South Tower, Entrance Lobby
1996
Wool and linen

This bold, colorful tapestry glorifying the fecundity of the natural world was designed and woven by Mollie Fletcher, who teaches at the College for Creative Studies. Born in Boston, Fletcher studied at the Rhode Island School of Design and the Cranbrook Academy of Art, and has created a number of other large-format tapestries, including one for the lobby of Ford Motor Credit, Inc., in Dearborn, Michigan. Apprenticed for five years to weaver Helena Hernmarck, Fletcher employs a technique in which she places a secondary weave on top of the ground weave to build greater dimensionality into her imagery.

Here, taking Michigan flowers and fauna as her subject, she composed a wall-filling, five-by-fifteen-foot weaving that portrays, in gigantic scale, a rose, lilies, tulips, and black-eyed susans, along with two butterflies and a moth that animate the blue zone of the sky. The two horizontal bands of blue and brown are counterpointed by the rhythmic deployment of the vertical stems and stalks and curvaceous blossoms and leaves of the flowers aligned in a row. The warm tones and profuse flowering of *Michigan Garden* soften and humanize the institutional architecture of the lobby area. Indeed, as the artist has affirmed, "It is my intention that the harmony and diversity . . . in nature is a visual symbol of hope for an ideal world."

F-7
The Echo of Flora Exotica
Gerhardt Knodel (b. 1940)
William Beaumont Hospital, 3601 West Twelve Mile Road,
Royal Oak, South Tower Lobby
2005
Fabric, ink, Mylar, and fluorescent lights

Gerhardt Knodel, internationally known fiber-installation artist and former director of the Cranbrook Academy of Art, conceived *The Echo of Flora Exotica* for the three-story lobby of the South Tower of William Beaumont Hospital. The glossy, sky-lit atrium, with its polished marble floors and hard-edged appearance, was ideal for Knodel's expert ability to soften and humanize daunting spaces. Here, the artist devised a tripartite piece on three discontinuous walls that jut out to enclose an elevator shaft.

Knodel's guiding concept—to create a healing garden and to explore the connections between nature and medicine—was crystallized by his discovery of the lush woodcuts of flowering plants by Ukrainian-born American artist Jacques Hnizdovsky (1915–1985). Knodel had Hnizdovsky's botanical images digitally scanned, enlarged, and color-printed onto three forty-by-fourteen lengths of fabric, which are mounted on the walls. Teeming with movement, resplendently colored, and voluptuous in form, they evoke medieval mille-fleur tapestries. Suspended three feet in front of these floral extravaganzas are translucent Mylar grids into which have been cut the names of thirty-six famed healers—Hippocrates, Pasteur, and Freud, among others. In this layered arrangement, the garden images behind and the names in front come only gradually into view. "Meaning," as Knodel offers, "is constructed slowly, like healing."

As an illustrative aside, a number of Hnizdovsky's woodcuts are on view adjacent to *Flora Exotica*, emphasizing not only Knodel's indebtedness to the artist but also inherent "echoes" between past and present, living and dead, and nature and the world of healers and physicians.

Floral Exotica is Knodel's second installation at Beaumont; his *Lifelines* (1994) animates the upper reaches of the hospital's Garden Court. Other fabric installations by the artist are in place at the American Center, Southfield, and at Congregation Shaarey Sedek, West Bloomfield.

F-8

Progression

Charles McGee (b. 1924)
William Beaumont Hospital, 3601 West Thirteen Mile Road,
Royal Oak, South Tower Concourse
2005
Painted aluminum

The zany, rhythmic shapes of Charles McGee's *Progression* appear to move swiftly across the twenty-five-foot width of this mural decoration. The work's stark, boldly contrasting black and white forms, punctuated by painted circles and polka dots as well as thick and thin stripes disposed vertically or horizontally, overwhelm even one's peripheral vision. This three-dimensional aluminum relief is a large-scale example of the "Noah's Ark" series that the artist initiated in the 1980s, in which he has used either a representational or abstract style. The Old Testament account of Noah's Ark and its deliverance from the Flood is, for McGee, an allegory of society's escape from imminent destruction so that human progress might continue. The artist has also likened the cataclysm of the Deluge to the Detroit riots of 1967, which also necessitated a fresh start in its aftermath.

McGee's multilayered installation at William Beaumont Hospital "speaks," the artist explains, "to the spirit of healing and renewal made possible through medical science." Twelve organic forms suggestive of microorganisms, chromosomes, and microbes interact and overlap with amorphous human figures. Nine black rhomboid panels denote the laboratories and research institutions that produce medicines. McGee has identified the syncopated rhythms of jazz as an influence on his sprightly, seemingly extemporaneous compositions. *Progression*'s propulsive dynamic, anchored by the familiar tale of Noah and the Ark, reveals how the artist has married ancient and modern to fruitful effect.

Born in South Carolina, McGee moved to Detroit in 1934. He later studied at the College for Creative Studies prior to attending the Escuela Massana and the School of Graphics in Barcelona, Spain. Over his long career, the scope of his art has encompassed charcoal drawings, mural paintings, mixed-media assemblages, and large-scale public sculpture. Other works by McGee are housed in a People Mover station (see A-36c), Detroit Receiving Hospital (B-4), and Henry Ford Hospital.

F-9
Celestial Walk
Beverly Fishman (b. 1955)
William Beaumont Hospital,
3601 West Thirteen Mile Road,
Royal Oak, South Tower Lobby
1998
Photo-based collage,
acrylic, and resin on wood

Beverly Fishman has headed the Painting Department and served as artist-in-residence at the Cranbrook Academy of Art since 1992. For over a decade, she has focused on two-dimensional installations. These expansive, multipart works may comprise anywhere from a half a dozen to more than one hundred components arrayed across a wall and may vary in length from six to fifty feet. Her photo-based images run the gamut from micro to macro, from invisible-to-the-naked-eye cellular bodies to the star-strewn vastness of the universe.

Celestial Walk, commissioned by the William Beaumont Hospital in 1998, displays many of these characteristics. Consisting of more than one hundred fifty units, ranging from one to fourteen inches in diameter, it is approximately forty-five feet wide. Fishman finds sources for her cosmic referents in books and on the Internet; here, she mounted images of planets, galaxies, the Milky Way, and nebulae on tondo-shaped wood discs, and then accented them with acrylic paint. As one proceeds from one end of the work to the other, as the title proposes, the colored roundels modulate from dense, murky blue-blacks on the left to whites and pale blues at the center to greens and midnight blues on the right. These subtle variations in hue suggest that a wide spectrum of color exists in what is often simply perceived as deep, dark space.

Deployed in no discernable pattern across the wall, these porthole views offer glimpses into the chilly immensity of the cosmos. And yet, in its hospital setting, this evocation of outer space can also offer a consoling, sobering perspective on the place of human life in the universe. *Celestial Walk* provides an antidote to the all-too-human obsession with the minutiae of daily existence, including the woes of ill health and suffering. "The circular shapes are windows, like the eye or a telescope," Fishman has observed, "revealing the changing qualities of life."

F-10
Sticker Woman
James Surls (b. 1943)
Neiman Marcus, Somerset Collection,
2705 West Big Beaver Road, Troy
1976
Wood and steel

This monumental, bristling sculpture was created by Texas artist James Surls relatively early in his career. After graduating from the Cranbrook Academy of Art in 1969, Surls returned to his native Texas, where he began to teach and develop his personal sculptural vocabulary of spiky, projecting shapes that frequently evoke human or animal forms. Here, the large-scale *Sticker Woman*, placed directly on the grass without a pedestal, seems, like a porcupine or prickly insect, to have paused to warn others away before striding off. Though Brobdingnagian in size, *Sticker Woman*'s resemblance to a primitive toy animal or even fetish may recall the efforts of an amateur woodworker. Alternatively, supported on eight sturdy, A-frame legs, it suggests a missile or battering ram.

The fearsomeness of this huge creature, which stands twenty feet tall and measures forty feet in length, is somewhat tempered by the textured surface and organic warmth of the pine wood timbers ("carved" by Surls with a chainsaw) that form its numerous appendages.

The plain brick exterior of the building's façade behind it makes *Sticker Woman*, installed in this location by the Neiman Marcus corporation in 1992, that much more alive, powerful, and daringly eccentric.

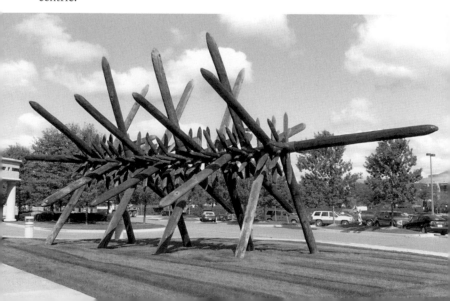

F-11
Reflective Head
Michael Ayrton (1921–1975)
Town Center and Civic Center Drives, Troy
1972
Bronze and reflective glass

Originally dominating the entrance court of Kmart International Headquarters in Troy, Michigan, Michael Ayrton's imposing *Reflective Head* (then known as *Corporate Head*) was given to the city when the corporation closed its office complex. In 2005, the city relocated the sculpture to a park-like setting on its civic campus.

Aryton's golden-hued colossus not only represents the external features of a human head but evokes the makeup of the human psyche as well. Two half heads, each facing in the opposite direction, are separated by a tall sheet of reflective glass. One looks toward an arc of trees, the other toward an expansive lawn. Moving around the solemn, serious heads, the viewer encounters several circular openings that reveal in turn smaller heads representing the many individuals who influence, guide, and shape us. As the artist has explained, "While the highest and the most important factor that any of us comprehend is the human head, it is through the conjunction of heads that human beings relate and combine to formulate concepts."

English sculptor Ayrton, who lived and worked in London, often combined contrasting materials to animate his figural compositions. Here, he incorporated bronze and reflective glass. The section that encompasses base, head, and mirror towers a full twenty-two feet; the height of the bronze heads is nine feet, while that of the reflective glass slab is fifteen.

When *Reflective Head* was relocated, a dedicatory plaque was added featuring a poem in three stanzas by Detroiter Craig Pangus (b. 1952). Included here are four lines that capture the intense concentration involved in decision making.

The present splits you down the middle
Half of you looking behind, and half, ahead.
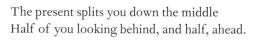
You clench your jaw, knit your brows
The neck's tendons stand out as taut cables.

F-12
Blue Chip
Lucius Carter (b. 1927)
HMS Products Company, 1200 East Big Beaver Road, Troy
1985
Painted steel

Lucius Carter's sculpture bends and spirals as it mounts to its full twelve-foot height. Commissioned by HMS Products, a machine tool builder, *Blue Chip*, according to artist and sculptor Carter, refers to the hot, curly scraps that are produced as metal is being cut on a machine at high speed. Moreover, the work's upward-moving form and title also function as a symbol for a progressive, high-quality "blue chip" business. The vividly hued, red-violet sculpture, with its angular, corkscrew shape, stands out in bold contrast to the cocoa-brown office and manufacturing building in front of which it is sited.

Born in Chicago, Carter lived and worked in Detroit for many years before moving to Florida in 1975, where he continues to reside.

F-13
Laura Sies Memorial
Robert Sestok (b. 1946)
Academy of the Sacred Heart, 1250 Kensington Road, Bloomfield Hills
2005
Bronze

Funded by the estate of Laura N. Sies, whose two granddaughters attended the Academy of the Sacred Heart, this memorial honors the alumnae of this educational institution (preschool through grade twelve), which was founded in 1851. Working from a design by Margaret Dawson, a 1997 graduate of the academy, Robert Sestok fabricated a four-and-one-half-foot tall stand of double-sided blossoming flowers held aloft on erect, cylindrical supports. Each of the four floral faces is unique. The view from both sides presents contrasting, stylized floral designs: one with angled shapes radiating from the center; the other with scalloped petals arranged around a circular core. That the blossoms are parallel to their supports rather than perpendicular to them underscores the outsized, ornamental forms. The bronze blooms, "planted" within a raised bed at the entrance to the academy's Field House, can be viewed easily from inside as well as outside. In lauding the educational growth of the school's many alumnae over the years, the *Laura Sies Memorial* also pays homage to the seasonal renewal of the school's verdant, wooded grounds, expressed by the sculpture's rich, green patina.

Recognized for his abstract steel sculptures, Sestok (see A-14, B-29) has also produced representational works, including landscape paintings, in the course of his career.

F-14
Sunglitter
Carl Milles (1875–1955)
Cranbrook Educational Community,
Academy Way and Lone Pine Road
1918
Bronze

During his first trip to America, in 1928, Carl Milles met George H. Booth (1864–1949), the founder of the Cranbrook Educational Community, who invited the Swedish sculptor to join the faculty of his newly formed experimental art school. Milles was resident sculptor at Cranbrook from 1931 to 1951. In 1934 the Cranbrook Foundation acquired from the artist a comprehensive collection of his work, the largest, in fact, outside Sweden. Placed in the sylvan setting of the Cranbrook grounds, the ninety pieces provide an unparalleled opportunity in America for study and appreciation of Milles's work. Milles returned to Sweden in 1951 and spent the last four years of his life in his beloved home, Lidingo.

In 1917 Milles adopted a highly stylized, elegant, and decorative manner that would characterize all of his mature work. *Sunglitter* was one of the first pieces he executed in this style and was always one of his favorites. It represents a naiad, or water nymph, riding a dolphin mounted on its base with a slim, curving support. Harriet Whitney Frishmuth's *Humoresque* (F-26) essays the same subject but to very different effect. Milles's dolphin and rider appear to be skimming at great speed across the water, their animated and vigorous silhouettes boldly outlined against the sky. So swift is their flight that the naiad's mouth has dropped open in fear, her hair flying in all directions, and she holds one hand to the back of her head, as if to steady herself, while grasping the forward fin of the slippery dolphin with the other. After the statue's theft in 2000, a replica was cast in 2002. A larger cast of this thirty-two-inch bronze is in the collection of the Detroit Institute of Arts.

F-15
Europa and the Bull
Carl Milles (1875–1955)
Cranbrook Educational Community, Triton Pool, Bloomfield Hills
1915–1916
Bronze

According to the Greek myth, the beautiful princess Europa was spotted bathing in the sea by the god Zeus, who transformed himself into a bull and carried her off to the island of Crete. For his sculpture, Carl Milles chose the moment when the bull, kneeling graciously, entices the princess to climb on his back. It is not clear whether the princess is innocently unaware that in a moment she will be carried off or is in fact a willing participant in the adventure. A serene and confident Europa, her drapery billowing out behind her, gingerly reaches forward to touch the tongue of the bull, whose massive bulk has been simplified into a crescent form. Designed by Milles as the central group of his *Europa Fountain* in Halmstad, Sweden, this cast dominates the northern edge of the Triton Pool.

The expansive, rectangular pool that steps down in graduated stages from the raised pedestal of *Europa* is populated by a bevy of bronzes including dolphins, various water creatures, and four life-size tritons (a kind of merman whose lower body metamorphoses into the tail of a fish). The tritons, dating from 1923–1924, strike animated poses while clutching large conical shells. Multiple sprays and arcs of water jet playfully from all members of this aquatic troupe gathered below the frolicking Europa and lusty bull.

The Triton Pool was completely rebuilt in 1998 to replicate the original 1939 design by Eliel Saarinen.

F-16
Jonah and the Whale
Carl Milles (1875–1955)
Cranbrook Educational Community, Jonah Pool, Bloomfield Hills
1932
Bronze

This humorous fountain sculpture overlooks a large pool shaped like a whale. The many jets and overflow basin provide an abundance of water for this antic piece, which lightheartedly interprets the Old Testament story of Jonah, who was swallowed and then later miraculously spit out by a whale. Water sprays from the whale's mouth; its tongue supports the two-foot, plump figure of Jonah. Water also jets from the mouths of twenty-four bronze fish swimming alongside. Sculptor Carl Milles has said, "It was the first thing I started here at Cranbrook. When I started it, I didn't know what to do, but I wanted to make a joke for the children. I thought it would be right to have Jonah appearing with a surprised look on his face." The fun-loving nature of the work, along with the erotic power of *Europa and the Bull* and the highly spiritual and intense *Orpheus Fountain* (F-15, F-17), demonstrate fully the range of expressive and decorative ideas of which Milles was capable.

F-17
Orpheus Fountain
Carl Milles (1875–1955)
Cranbrook Educational Community, Bloomfield Hills,
North of Art Museum Peristyle
1936
Bronze

In 1928 Carl Milles placed first in a competition for a fountain to be erected in front of the Stockholm Concert Hall, with a design of a thirty-eight-foot figure of Orpheus. During an eight-year delay in construction, Milles added eight life-size standing figures around the base of the colossal Orpheus. The *Orpheus Fountain* at Cranbrook is composed of casts of these eight male and female figures surrounded by a basin of water about twenty-five feet in diameter, and in a circular composition that lacks the central, towering Orpheus. Nevertheless, each of these attenuated, somewhat androgynous forms reveals his or her response to Orpheus's celestial music. All eight figures lean slightly forward off their supports, which are stylized branches, as if straining to catch the tantalizing sound of Orpheus's magical lyre. Straining harder than the rest is Beethoven, the only figure identified by Milles, his head thrown back and arms upraised in a gesture of intense involvement. The absence of Orpheus here only seems to add to the haunting effect of his ethereal melodies on this ensemble of figures.

F-18
Cranbrook Ingathering
Bernard (Tony) Rosenthal (b. 1914)
Cranbrook Educational Community, Bloomfield Hills,
Adjacent to Art Museum Parking Lot
1980
Cor-ten steel

Tony Rosenthal is represented by two dark-red, Cor-ten steel sculptures at Cranbrook, including the spacious twenty-five-by-twenty-seven-foot, house-size *Cranbrook Ingathering* and the compact, six-foot-tall *T-Square* (located south of the Peristyle). Now a New Yorker, the Illinois-born sculptor trained at the Cranbrook Academy of Art with Carl Milles in the late 1930s. Another Rosenthal sculpture in the area is a fifteen-foot-high rotating cube on the campus of the University of Michigan, where the artist also studied.

Sited on a gently sloping, grassy plot (about the size of a modest residential lot) and backdropped by a screen of trees, *Cranbrook Ingathering,* as its title implies, invites one to walk within its three-roomed interior. Though sans roof, this partial-walled "house" offers protected, private enclosure as well as views to the outside, including the adjacent parking lot. The walls and "furnishings" for the trio of rooms are a result of Rosenthal's inventive use of basic two- and three-dimensional geometric forms—rectangles, triangles, and hollow columns or beams. Cut to different lengths and deployed horizontally or vertically, the hollow columns serve as bench or table; the tallest, at ten-and-a-half feet, might even be read as "chimney." The largest chamber contains a two-foot-high circular well or basin intimating hearth and community. Indeed, in all seasons, whether one is sunning oneself in warm weather or taking shelter from the cold, *Cranbrook Ingathering* radiates a welcoming aura.

The sculpture, on extended loan from Lois Spector Freeman and Alan Freeman, exemplifies, along with works by Mark di Suvero (F-19), Michael D. Hall (see F-25), Richard Nonas (see B-10), and Peter Voulkos, the abstract aesthetic of the later twentieth century in the Cranbrook collection.

F-19
For Mother Teresa
Mark di Suvero (b. 1933)
Cranbrook Educational Community, Bloomfield Hills,
Northwest of Art Museum Peristyle
1998
Painted steel, stainless steel, and steel

Internationally renowned sculptor Mark di Suvero seems most at home creating architecturally scaled works of art. Like many pieces by this artist, *For Mother Teresa* is monumental: it towers sixty feet aboveground and has a horizontal reach of half that dimension. Constructed of steel components displaying three contrasting sur-

faces, the work includes an eye-catching suspended element that, as in a mobile, is activated by air or wind currents. From near the top of the steeply angled, fire-engine red superstructure dangles a sleek, stainless-steel configuration that by turns evokes ears, wings, fins, Möbius strip, plow, or even an elaborate, swept-back headdress. Its height and movement are offset by the rusty steel, box-within-a-box extrusion situated on the ground between two of the piece's I-beams.

Named for Mother Teresa (1910–1997), whom the Catholic Church has beatified for her selfless devotion to improving life in the slums of Calcutta, the sculpture is among numerous di Suveros honoring individuals of cultural or humanitarian significance. In addition to the "angel of mercy," as the nun has been described by fellow social workers, the sculptor has created pieces to celebrate poet Marianne Moore, singer Billie Holiday, and composers Beethoven, Handel, and Vivaldi. While the shiny form embodying Mother Teresa's lofty vision and her inspiring achievement floats high above, the rusty brown boxes nestled below the red tower are reminders that noble actions often take place within harsh, unrefined environments.

Born in Shanghai, di Suvero grew up in San Francisco and attended the University of California–Berkeley before moving to New York in 1957. Currently, he divides his time between studios in California, France, and New York.

A major addition to the Cranbrook collection, *For Mother Teresa* was presented in 2005 by Margo V. Cohen as a commemorative gift in honor of Maurice Cohen.

F-20
Upcast
Clement Meadmore (1929–2005)
West Maple and Southfield Roads,
Birmingham
1987
Painted aluminum

After graduating from the Royal Melbourne Institute of Technology, Australian-born Clement Meadmore moved to New York in 1963, arriving just at the moment when the emotional, gestural idiom of the Abstract Expressionists (Jackson Pollock, Franz Kline, et al.) intersected with the angular, geometric formulas of Minimalists Donald Judd, Tony Smith (B-7), and others. Rather than rejecting the earlier style, Meadmore, in his first major sculptures of the late 1960s, combined the fluid, "drawn" character of gestural abstraction with the reductive rigor of geometric abstraction.

In conversations about his art, the artist frequently speaks about his intention to "transcend geometry." To do so, he often combines, as in *Upcast*, a cube and a quarter circle to create dynamic forms that seem to move weightlessly into the air from a single support or "leg." The squared tube from which *Upcast* rises is just fourteen inches on a side. As it ascends, the matte-black sculpture takes off in one direction and then lunges in another. From one side, it looks like a switchback road climbing uphill. The topmost shape—a blunt, rectangular form—seems to defy gravity and release the pent-up tension created by the diverging elements below. The sculpture's opposing projections ensure another of Meadmore's aims: to "avoid the feeling of a front and back." Thus, installed at a busy intersection, *Upcast* not only inhabits its small triangular plot but boldly asserts its three-dimensionality from all directions. Collectors Frederick and Barbara Erb donated the sculpture to Birmingham for the city's enhancement.

Meadmore became a U.S. citizen in 1973 and lived in New York until his death. His sculptures have been widely collected both in the United States (including, in Michigan, the Detroit Institute of Arts and the Dennos Museum Center in Traverse City) and abroad, namely Australia and Japan.

F-21

The Freedom of the Human Spirit

Marshall Fredericks (1908–1998)
Shain Park, Bates and Merrill Streets, Birmingham
1964
Bronze

As if defying gravity, a man, woman, and three geese lift off from the center of a circular fountain in this downtown park. The sleek, streamlined birds seem to strain as they thrust themselves into the air, while the two figures appear to rise up effortlessly, as if simply raising their arms above their heads allows them to soar aloft. And indeed, as the title proposes, the human spirit, which these idealized figures represent, is able to fly despite the earthbound nature of the human body.

Structurally, what actually support the "flight" of figures and fowl are the four pointed, spike-like shapes that abstractly reference the organic vegetation from which both game and the unfettered human spirit take flight.

Marshall Fredericks's lofty, darkly patinated, twenty-five-foot-high bronze not only dominates the park but also summarizes one of the preeminent goals—the freedom of the human spirit—of communities across the land. The sculptor's spirited depictions of human striving can also be seen in downtown Detroit (A-24) and in Royal Oak (F-3).

F-22
City of Southfield
Mel Leiserowitz (b. 1925)
Southfield Civic Center, 26000 Evergreen Road, Southfield
1983
Painted steel

Crowning the top of a low hillock on the grounds of the Southfield Civic Center is Mel Leiserowitz's *City of Southfield*. This brightly painted steel sculpture, commissioned by the city of Southfield in 1982, was originally installed within the outdoor courtyard of the civic center building, where it was surrounded by the glass, metal, and brick walls of the complex. The artist has expressed satisfaction with the work's relocation to its present, pastoral site. Born in Iowa, where he studied at the University of Iowa, Leiserowitz joined the art faculty at Michigan State University and taught there for many years.

Leiserowitz's *City of Southfield* was assembled from five narrow, bent or curved sheets of steel painted in hues of magenta and royal and light blue. Two low-lying shapes support the three gracefully curving forms that overlap and rise to a height of fifteen feet. The structure of the sculpture suggests convergence; while abstract, *City of Southfield* is a symbol of unity for a community that encompasses a diversity of people, beliefs, and forces.

F-23
Drifter
Michael D. Hall (b. 1940)
Lawrence Technological University, 21000 West Ten Mile Road, Southfield
1977
Painted aluminum

Sited in a tree-circled clearing on the campus of Lawrence Technological University, Michael D. Hall's *Drifter*, as the title implies, does
indeed seem to be gently drifting or settling to earth. Constructed
of gray, painted struts, braces, and sheet aluminum, the thirty-three-
by-forty-three-foot tilted plane appears almost to float in space. Like
a fragment of a large industrial structure (a bridge, trestle, or over-
pass) that has been abandoned in mid-construction or left to dete-
riorate, *Drifter* seems to be in a state of collapse, as if sinking slowly
into the ground. At the same time, it recalls a roofed structure (it is
seventeen feet tall at its highest corner) offering shelter to viewers
who walk through and under it.

Originally assembled in the Detroit Institute of Arts for an exhibition in 1977, *Drifter* was reconstructed at Lawrence in 1996 when
it was donated to the university by David and Doreen Hermelin.
Hall's characteristic idiom of industrial forms and materials seems
particularly appropriate for a technological university.

California-born Hall studied at the University of North Carolina and the University of Washington before settling in the Detroit
area in 1970, where he directed the Sculpture Department at the
Cranbrook Academy of Art from 1970 to 1990.

F-24
Stargazer
(for Columbus Cain)
Michael D. Hall (b. 1940)
Galleria Office Centre,
27700 Northwestern Highway,
Southfield
1983
Painted steel

Michael D. Hall's romanti-
cally titled *Stargazer (for
Columbus Cain)* dominates
the entrance to this broad,
sprawling, three-story complex. Placed on a perpendicular axis three hundred feet
from the office building's
entrance, the sculpture's
two fifty-foot "walls" form
a screen to shield one from
the busy highway beyond.
The interior walls of *Stargazer* are painted sky blue
to simulate the sky, and the
many tiny openings within the walls mimic twinkling stars. Constructed from triangular steel plates bolted to a network of supports,
the pierced walls of *Stargazer* frame a semi-enclosed observatory
for the spectator, while the natural sky in effect creates a third, star-
studded wall, as Hall's seemingly unfinished structure merges seam-
lessly with the sky beyond. The subtitle in fact links the explorer
Christopher Columbus and the biblical Cain, who wandered in the
desert for many years. The segmented components of *Stargazer* are
analogous to the gridded façade of blue and pink tinted glass as well
as to the stepped roofline of the building's design.

In contrast to *Stargazer*'s black exterior (as viewed from the highway), the surprise of its expansive cerulean blue interior attests to
Hall's ability to turn obdurate industrial materials to expressive effect. A similar handling may be seen in other of the sculptor's works
in the area (F-23, F-25).

F-25
Covington
Michael D. Hall (b. 1940)
30833 Northwestern Highway, Farmington Hills
1972
Painted aluminum

Michael D. Hall (see also F-23, F-24), uses simple architectural components—braces, struts, steel, and aluminum—to create pure, abstract shapes. At the same time, however, his forms relate to the rural Midwestern landscape, with its gates, fences, pipelines, storage tanks, barriers, and billboards. *Covington,* on extended loan from art patrons Gilbert and Lila Silverman, is one of a series Hall began in 1969 of gates or fence-like constructions named after small towns. Meticulously crafted and carefully painted white, *Covington* nevertheless evokes a collapsing segment of a gate. Its poignant isolation and seeming abandonment betray a romanticism one might not expect from an artist who once described himself as "The Sculptor of Interstate 75."

Hall is well represented in metropolitan Detroit in both suburban and urban locations. *Covington,* as well as *Drifter, Stargazer,* and an architectonic structure titled *Amaranth* at Cranbrook (see F-18) are in suburban settings. Two works by the sculptor are located in the city's midtown cultural district, including a piece from the permanent collection of the Detroit Institute of Arts on display in the Josephine F. Ford Sculpture Garden (see B-10).

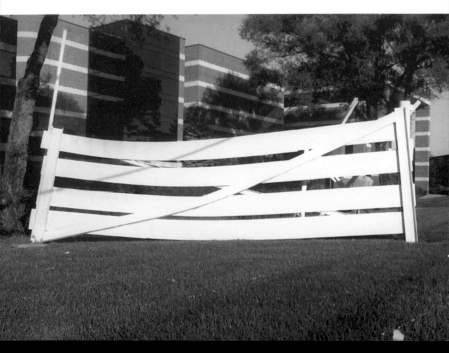

F-26
Humoresque
Harriet Whitney Frishmuth (1880–1980)
Farmington Community Library, 32737 West Twelve Mile Road,
Farmington Hills
1924
Bronze

Set into a square, shallow, reflecting pool of recent vintage, this early twentieth-century fountain sculpture by Harriet Whitney Frishmuth seems the embodiment of youthful, sensual enjoyment. The lithe nude of *Humoresque* is poised on toe on the back of a fish whose tail caresses her calf as she nuzzles its open mouth. Seven feet tall and cast in bronze, the green patinated figure flings out one arm to maintain her balance on the speeding fish while grasping another fish on her shoulder. She smiles and her windblown hair flies back as her body spirals athletically into space.

Known for her bronzes of exuberant nudes, Frishmuth was born in Philadelphia and studied in France before beginning her sculpture career. Settling in 1908 in New York, where she lived until 1937, she often employed dancers as her models since, as she explained, "Most of my figures express motion . . . [and] some of the poses can only be held a moment." A favorite model often struck poses as music played; indeed, the title of the work included here refers to a fanciful musical composition, a description that pertains to the sculpture as well.

Originally commissioned for a garden in upstate New York, this cast of *Humoresque* was donated to the City of Farmington Hills by Dr. Allen Zieger in 1976.

Epilogue

I would like to describe *Art in Detroit Public Places* as the definitive guide to public art in metropolitan Detroit, but reality suggests that this text will be out of date even before publication (and no matter how often it is subsequently revised). Works of public art are in fact far more mobile, fragile, and ephemeral than these seemingly solid monuments at first suggest. One can cite the long ago loss of the colossal statue of Constantine from Roman times that survives in fragments and the industrious transport over the centuries of Egyptian obelisks from country to country as evidence of the contingent nature of public art. In our own region a cursory comparison of the two previous incarnations of this book with the present one reveals the often little-noted changes and losses—as well as additions—that are the lot of public art objects.

Presently, in 2008, the last new entry to make it under the wire and into the book is David Barr's *Dawn*, and with equal dispatch the text on Alexander Calder's *Jeune fille et sa suite*, which twice anchored the cover of the guide, was tweaked to reflect its two-mile journey north from a downtown corner to the Cultural Center. Perhaps too, the next time around, the park at Twelfth and Clairmont Streets that provides the setting for Jack Ward's untitled sculpture marking the site of the starting point of the 1967 "riot" will be sufficiently restored and presentable to warrant inclusion.

Thus, the actual writing of the book that will be published in mid-2008 will have been completed in mid-2007. So, as I write this in September 2007, nine months before the third *Art in Detroit Public Places* rolls off the presses, I expect to be just as curious as you to note what changes in the landscape of public art will have taken place between now and then and in the years to come as well.

Suggestions for Further Reading

Art in Public Places: A Survey of Community-Sponsored Projects Supported by the National Endowment for the Arts. Washington, DC: Partners for Livable Places, 1981.

Artists in Michigan, 1900–1976: A Biographical Dictionary. Detroit: Wayne State University Press, 1989.

Bach, Ira J., and Mary Lackritz Gray. *A Guide to Chicago's Public Sculpture.* Chicago: University of Chicago Press, 1983.

Basa, Lynn. *The Artist's Guide to Public Art: How to Find and Win Commissions.* New York: Allworth, 2008.

Bogart, Michelle H. *Public Sculpture and the Civic Ideals in New York City, 1890–1930.* Washington, DC: Smithsonian Institution Press, 1997.

Boileau, Lowell. "The Fabulous Ruins of Detroit." 1996. http://www.detroityes.com/webisodes.htm.

Carducci, Vincent. "Res Publica, Detroit Style." November 25, 2003. http://www.thedetroiter.com/OCT03/publicsculpture.html.

Clark-Langager, Sarah A. *Sculpture in Place: A Campus as Site.* Bellingham: Western Washington University, 2002.

Clements, David. *Talking Shops: Detroit Commercial Folk Art.* Detroit: Wayne State University Press, 2005.

Cockcroft, Eva, John Weber, and Jim Cockcroft. *Toward a People's Art: The Contemporary Mural Movement.* New York: E. P. Dutton, 1977.

Connecting the Dots: Tyree Guyton's Heidelberg Project. Detroit: Wayne State University Press, 2007.

Conner, Janis, and Joel Rosenkranz. *Rediscoveries in American Sculpture: 1893–1939.* Austin: University of Texas Press, 1989.

Coonerty, Ryan. *Etched in Stone: Enduring Words from Our Nation's Monuments.* Washington, D.C.: National Geographic Society, 2007.

Doezema, Marianne, and June Hargrove. *The Public Monument and Its Audience.* Cleveland: Cleveland Museum of Art, 1977.

Doss, Erika. *Spirit Poles and Flying Pigs: Public Art and Cultural Democracy in American Communities.* Washington, DC: Smithsonian Institution Press, 1995.

Doty, Robert. *Project: New Urban Monuments.* Akron, OH: Akron Art Institute, 1977.

Eckert, Kathryn Bishop. *Cranbrook: The Campus Guide.* New York: Princeton Architectural Press, 2001.

Elsen, Albert E. *Rodin's* Thinker *and the Dilemmas of Modern Public Sculpture.* New Haven: Yale University Press, 1985.

Farley, Reynolds, and Judy Mullin. "Detroit: The History and Future of the Motor City." 2005. http://detroit1701.org.

Finkelpearl, Tom. *Dialogues in Public Art.* Cambridge, MA: MIT Press, 2000.

Finn, David. *How to Look at Sculpture.* New York: Harry N. Abrams, 1989.

Fredericks, Suzanne, P. *Marshall M. Fredericks, Sculptor.* University Center, MI: Marshall M. Fredericks Sculpture Museum, Saginaw Valley State University; Detroit: Wayne State University Press, 2003.

Fundaburk, Emma L., and Thomas G. Davenport. *Art in Public Places in the United States.* Bowling Green, OH: Bowling Green University Popular Press, 1975.

Gerdts, William H. *American Neo-Classic Sculpture.* New York: Viking, 1973.

Goldwater, Robert. *What Is Modern Sculpture?* New York: Museum of Modern Art, 1969.

Gooding, Mel. *Public: Art: Space.* Seattle: University of Washington Press, 1998.

Hendry, Fay L. *Outdoor Sculpture in Grand Rapids.* Okemos, MI: iota, 1980.

An Inspirational Body of Work: The Fine Art of Blue Cross Blue Shield of Michigan. Detroit: Blue Cross Blue Shield of Michigan, 2003.

Jacob, Mary Jane, Michael Brenson, and Eva M. Olson. *Culture in Action: A Public Art Program of Sculpture Chicago.* Seattle: Bay, 1995.

Keller, Martha, and Michael J. Curtis. *Public Art in Ann Arbor and Washtenaw County.* Ann Arbor, MI: Alexa Lee Gallery, 1995.

Kwon, Miwon. *One Place after Another: Site-Specific Art and Locational Identity.* Cambridge, MA: MIT Press, 2002.

Lacy, Suzanne, ed. *Mapping the Terrain: New Genre Public Art.* Seattle: Bay, 1995.

Levinson, Sanford. *Written in Stone: Public Monuments in Changing Societies.* Durham: Duke University Press, 1998.

Marback, Richard. "Unclenching the Fist: Embodying Rhetoric and Giving Objects Their Due." *Rhetoric Society Quarterly* (forthcoming 2008).

Marling, Karal Ann. *Wall-to-Wall America: A Cultural History of Post-Office Murals in the Great Depression.* Minneapolis: University of Minnesota Press, 1982.

Miles, Malcolm. *Art, Space and the City: Public Art and Urban Futures.* New York: Routledge, 1997.

Monuments and Sculptures in Detroit. Detroit Historical Museum, 2004. http://www.detroithistorical.org/collections/vewebsite2/exhibit3/vexmain3.htm.

Outdoor Sculpture in Kalamazoo. Okemos, MI: iota, 1980.

Outdoor Sculpture in Lansing. Okemos, MI: iota, 1980.

Pasternak, Ann. *Creative Time: The Book.* Princeton: Princeton Architectural Press, 2007.

Patrimonio: The Legacy of Italian Art in Michigan. Detroit: Wayne State University Department of Art and Art History, 1996.

Plummer, Ellen A., and Frederick W. Mayer. *Outdoor Sculpture: The University of Michigan Ann Arbor Campus.* Ann Arbor: University of Michigan Museum of Art, 1993.

Raven, Arlene. *Art in the Public Interest.* Ann Arbor, MI: UMI Research Press, 1989.

Redstone, Louis G. *Art in Architecture.* New York: McGraw-Hill, 1968.

Redstone, Louis G., and Ruth R. Redstone. *Public Art: New Directions.* New York: McGraw-Hill, 1981.

Reynolds, Donald M. *Masters of American Sculpture: The Figurative Tradition from the American Renaissance to the Millennium.* New York: Abbeville, 1993.

Robinette, Margaret A. *Outdoor Sculpture: Object and Environment.* New York: Watson-Guptill Publications, 1976.

Rubenstein, Charlotte S. *American Women Sculptors.* Boston: G. K. Hall and Company, 1990.

Savage, Kirk. *Standing Soldiers, Kneeling Slaves: Race, War, and Monument in Nineteenth-Century America.* Princeton: Princeton University Press, 1997.

Sculpture at Cranbrook, 1978–1980. Bloomfield Hills, MI: Cranbrook Academy of Art Museum, 1980.

Sculpture Off the Pedestal. Grand Rapids, MI: Grand Rapids Art Museum, 1973.

Selections from the Wayne State University Art Collection. Detroit: Wayne State University, 1992.

Senie, Harriet F. *Contemporary Public Sculpture: Tradition, Transformation, and Controversy.* New York: Oxford University Press, 1992.

Senie, Harriet F., and Sallie Webster. *Critical Issues in Public Art.* New York: Harper Collins, 1993.

Smith, Bob and Roberta. *Art U Need: My Part in the Public Art Revolution.*

London: Black Dog, 2007.

Stokes, Charlotte. *Bronze Ladies, Corporate Giants, Saints and Sinners: Public Art in Oakland County.* Rochester, MI: Oakland University Odyssey Research Monographs, 1991.

Symmes, Marilyn, ed. *Fountains: Splash and Spectacle. Water and Design from the Renaissance to the Present.* New York: Rizzoli International Publications, and Cooper-Hewitt, National Design Museum, Smithsonian Institution, 1998.

Thalacker, Donald W., ed. *The Place of Art in the World of Architecture.* Ann Arbor, MI: Chelsea House/Bowker, 1980.

Walt, Irene. *Art in the Stations: The Detroit People Mover.* Detroit Art in the Stations, 2004.

Index

Note: Titles of works are italicized

Abstract Expressionism, 207
ABZ—Everything Is Anything (Piet),
    124
Academy of Sacred Heart, 23, 197
Acconci, Vito, xvii
Adams, Herbert: *James Scott Memorial
    Fountain* (with Gilbert), 111–12
Alger, Russell A. Memorial Fountain
    (French and Bacon), 14
Allen, Richard, 137
Allied Signal Automotive Sector, 60
Ambassador Bridge, 144
Amelia Earhart Middle School, 147
An American Lightbow (Scarff),
    96–97
Andonian, Michelle, 186
Antonakas, Stephen, 52
Anton Art Center, Mt. Clemens, 169,
    172
Apel, Karl, 62
Arch: Montrose (Linburg), 77
Archipenko, Alexander, 105
Arc (Pancioli), 63–64
Arman (Armand Fernandez):

Untitled, 158
Art in Public Places program, xvi
Art in the Stations, Detroit People
    Mover, 52–55
Ascension (Lehr), 139
Atheneum Hotel, 46, 76
Austen, Hartmut, 181
Automotive Mural (Gropper), 87
Ayrton, Michael: *Reflective Head*,
    xvii, 194–95

Babcock, Herb: *Monroe Monument
    Marker* (with Ernstberger), 6;
    Woodward Monument Marker
    (with Ernstberger), 6
Bacon, Henry: *Russell A. Alger
    Memorial Fountain*, 14
Baden-Powell, Sir Robert, 136
Bakker, Dirk, 186
Bambara of Mali, 65
Barbour, Levi L. Memorial Fountain
    (Fredericks), xv, 114–15
Barr, David, 182; *Crystal
    Transformation*, 165, 166; *Dawn,*

223

Barr, David (*continued*)
164–65, 217; *Transcending*, 23, 33–35, 42, 165
Base Line (Eight Mile Road), 166
BASF Waterfront Park, 25, 152–53
Baskin, Gere, 148
Beasley, Bruce: *Six-Tonner for Julian*, 174
Beaumont Hospital, Royal Oak. *See* William Beaumont Hospital, Royal Oak
Beaux-Arts style, 14, 66, 112
Belle Isle, xiv; Central Avenue, 9, 116, 117, 118, 119, 120; Formal Garden West of Conservatory, 114–15; Lakeside and Riverbank Drives, 121; map of, 100; Western end, 111–12, 113
Beltchenko, Mark, xvi; *"Artist Type" Personality*, 141; *Type "A" Personality*, 141; *Type "B" Personality*, 141
Bendix Corporation, 60
Bennett, Richard: *Gazelle*, 121; *Geome-Tree* (with Corbin), 138; *Mermaid*, 121; *Sentry*, 65; *Waves*, 121
Bertoia, Harry, 62
Big Fish (Valdez), 145
Billboard, 180–81
Birmingham, 207, 208–9
Blake, Matthew: *Millennium Bell*, 15
Bloomfield Hills, 197–206
Blue Chip (Carter), 196
Blue Cross, Blue Shield of Michigan complex, xvi, 21–22, 24–25
The Blue Nile (McGee), 53
Blum, Andrea: *Environmental Sculpture*, 160–61
Boll Family YMCA, xvi, 70, 141
Bonner, Thomas N., 86
Booth, George H., 198
Booth, Ralph H., 43
Borglum, Gutzon, xiv; *Lincoln, Abraham*, 43
Boy Scout (McKenzie), 136
Boy Scouts of America Headquarters, Detroit Area Council, 136

Brady, James J. Memorial (Cashwan and O'Dell), 9, 117
Brancusi, Constantin, 108
Bresee, Mikel, 76
Broadway station, Detroit People Mover, 53
Brose, Morris, 125; *Sentinel X*, 10, 11
"Brother Sun, Sister Moon," 109
Burns, Robert (Lawson), 58, 59
Burst (Katz), 176–77
Byars, Chris: *Untitled*, 159

Cadillac, Marquette, LaSalle, and Richard (Melchers), 82–83
Cadillac Center Station, Detroit People Mover, 52
Cadillac Memorial Gardens-East, 173
Calder, Alexander, xiv, 62, 72; *Jeune fille et sa suite (Young Woman and Her Suitors)*, 68–69, 217; mobile, 69, 126; *The X and Its Tails*, 69
Calder stabile, xvi
Campus Martius, xv, 5, 64
Capitol Park, 10
Capuchin Order, 109
The Carnival! (Piet), 102
Caro, Anthony, 72
Carousel (Stoltz), 104
Carter, Lucius: *Blue Chip*, 196
Casey, Solanus, 109
Cashwan, Samuel, 125; *James J. Brady Memorial* (with O'Dell), 9, 117
Cass Corridor artists, 23
Cass Park, 58, 59
Cavanaugh, Jerome, 30
Celestial Walk (Fishman), 192
Chamberlain, John: *Deliquescence*, xvii, 48
Charles H. Wright Museum of African American History, 46, 65, 76, 121, 138
Charlie, Inuk, 182
Chatelain, James, 150
Chavez, Cesar, 35
Chene Park, 18, 102, 176
Chesney, Edward: *Father Clement Kern*, 133
Children's Museum, 94–95

City of Detroit Recreation Department, xv
City of Southfield (Leiserowitz), 210
Clark Park Sculpture Project, 147–49
Coasting the Base Line (Barr), 166
Cobo Center, 36
Cobo Center Garage, 145
Cohen, Margo V., xv, 206
Cohen, Maurice, 206
Coleman A. Young Municipal Center, xiv
College for Creative Studies, xvii, 77; parking structure, 75–76
Color Cubes (Rubello), 51
Columbus, Christopher (Rivalta), 27
Comerica Building, 18, 117
Compuware Corporation Headquarters, 64
"Connections" Bridge, 76
Continuity (Lowery), 86
Continuity Tower (Sestok), 98–99, 150
Contreras, Johnny Bear: *Sister Earth*, 109
Cooley, Phillip, 134
Corbin, Matt: *Geome-Tree* (and Bennett), 138
Corktown, 132, 133
The Corn Field (Valdez and Puntigam), 145–46
County Seat (Kulak), 169–70
Court, Caroline Blessing Browne, 186; *Penelopeia*, 142–43
Covenant (Timlin), 108
Covington (Hall), 213
Cram, Joyce, 186
Cranbrook Educational Community, xiv, 73, 198–99, 200–201, 202, 203, 204, 205
Cranbrook Ingathering (Rosenthal), 204
Creation Garden (various artists), 109
Crowley, Tim and Kathy, 108
Cruz, Arturo, 144
Crystal Transformation (Barr), 165, 166
Cultural Center, map of art, 56
Curved Form with Rectangle and Space (Teicher), 70–71

The Dance of Life (Smith, Ann F.), 106
Dancing Hands (Sestok), 21–22, 150
Dante Alighieri (Romanelli), 119, 120
Dawn (Barr), 164–65, 217
Dawson, Margaret, 197
Dearborn, 156, 157, 158, 159
DeBaptiste, George, 31
De Giusti, Sergio, 35; *General Anthony Wayne*, 89; *Transcending*, 23, 33–35, 42, 165; *Urban Stele*, 22–23
DeLauro, Joseph N.: *Exploration*, 80–81
Deliquescence (Chamberlain), xvii, 48
DeLue, Donald: *George Washington*, 28
Detroit, downtown (map), 3
Detroit Athletic Club, 76
Detroit Cultural Center, Josephine F. Ford Sculpture Garden, xvii, 72, 74, 213
Detroit Industry frescos (Rivera), 87
Detroit Institute of Arts, xvii, xviii, 66, 67, 68–69, 104, 198
Detroit Lions Academy, 125
Detroit Metropolitan Airport, Michael Berry International Terminal, 44
Detroit New Morning (Loving), 54
Detroit People Mover, *Art in the Stations*, 52–55
Detroit Public Library, 78, 79, 80, 112; Campbell Branch, 145
Detroit Receiving Hospital and University Center, Art in, xv, 55, 62–64, 186
Detroit Renaissance, xv
Detroit riots of 1967, xv, 190, 218
Detroit 300, xv, 31
Detroit 300 Conservancy, 6
Detroit Symphony Orchestra, Orchestra Place courtyard, 60–61
Detroit Zoological Park, 141, 182
Dinan, John D., 168
di Suvero, Mark: *For Mother Teresa*, 205–6
Diversity Is Our Strength, 144

Dodge, Anna Thomson, 30
Dodge, Horace, Jr., 30
Dodge, Horace E., and Son Memorial Fountain (Noguchi), 30
Dodge, Mrs. Horace C., xv
Dolega, Stanley, 103; *Untitled*, 113
Donaldson, John M., 83
Drifter (Hall), 211
DTE Energy, 6
Duchamp-Villon, Raymond, 72
Duffy, Edward W. and Company, 150
Duffy, James F., Jr., 150
Dunikowski, Xaver: *Count Casimir Pulaski*, 151
Dwight, Ed: *International Memorial to the Underground Railroad*, 31–32

Eastern Market Murals (Pollack), 127
Ebel, Larry, 52
The Echo of Flora Exotica (Knodel), 188–89
Edward W. Duffy and Company, 150
Elmwood Cemetery, xiv, 107
Elmwood Park Plaza, 103, 104, 113
Employees Park, William Beaumont Hospital, Royal Oak, 186
The Entrance (Piet), 18
Environmental Sculpture (Blum), 160–61
Erb, Frederick and Barbara, 207
Ernstberger, Eric: *Monroe Monument Marker* (with Babcock), 6; *Woodward Monument Marker* (with Babcock), 6
Europa and the Bull (Milles), 200–201
Europa Fountain, Halmstad, Sweden (Milles), 201
Expanding Passage (McGillis et al.), 148, 149
Exploration (DeLauro), 80–81

Fairlane Town Center, Dearborn, 158, 159
Fallen Timbers, battle of, 89
Fanfare (Stoltz), 104
Farmington Community Library, 214–15
Farmington Hills, 213, 214–15

Feigenson, Jacqueline, 99
Ferndale, 180–81
Ferretti, Jerome: *Mural*, 132, 135
Ferry, W. Hawkins, 93, 126
Fishman, Beverly: *Celestial Walk*, 192
"The Fist" (*Memorial to Joe Louis*), 36–37
Flaherty, Kevin C. Memorial (Massey), 46–47
Fletcher, Mollie: *Michigan Garden*, 187
Flight of the Spirit (*Waterman Monument*) (Rogers), 107
Ford, Henry (Fredericks), 156
Ford Centennial Library, 156, 186
Ford Community and Performing Arts Center, 157
Ford Motor Credit, Inc., 187
Ford Sculpture Garden, Detroit Cultural Center. *See* Josephine F. Ford Sculpture Garden, Detroit Cultural Center
Ford Underground Garage, 132
Ford Wyandotte Hospital, 186
For Mother Teresa (di Suvero, Mark), 205–6
Fort/Cass station, Detroit People Mover, 55
Francis of Assisi, Saint, 109
Frankel, Nancy: *Sister Moon*, 109
Fredericks, Marshall, 43, 52, 137, 153, 182; bust of John Fitzgerald Kennedy, 169; *The Freedom of the Human Spirit*, 208–9; *Henry Ford*, 156; *Levi L. Barbour Memorial Fountain*, 114–15, 121; *The Spirit of Detroit*, 38–39; *Star Dream*, 183; *Victory Eagle and Pylons*, 42
Freedman, Marcia, 62
Freedom House, 144
The Freedom of the Human Spirit (Fredericks), 208–9
Freeman, Lois Spector and Alan, 204
French, Daniel Chester, 5, 13, 14, 50, 118; *Russell A. Alger Memorial Fountain*, 14
Friends of Belle Isle, xvii

Friends of Modern and
  Contemporary Art, 67
Frishmuth, Harriet Whitney:
  Humoresque, 198, 214–15
funerary art, xiv
Funnel Project (Randall, Holm, and
  Newbold), 134

Gabriel Richard Park, 110
Galbreath, Lynn, 62
Galileo's Night Vision (Wesner and
  Storm), 171–72
Galleria Office Centre, Southfield,
  212
Gateway to Freedom (Dwight), 31
Gazelle (Bennett), 121
General Motors Technical Center, 165
General Motors World Headquarters,
  29, 47, 132
Geome-Tree (Bennett and Corbin),
  138
Gilbert, Cass: *James Scott Memorial
  Fountain* (with Adams), 111–12
Gilliam, Sam, xiv; *Wave Composition*,
  62, 63
Giuliano, Vincenzo, 27
Glacial (Rutzky), 167
Gomidas (Tchakmakchian), 41
Goody, Dick, 62
Gracehoper (Smith), 67
Grace Hospital, Webber Memorial
  Building, 44
Graham, Robert, xiv; *Louis, Joe,
  Memorial to*, 36–37
Grand Circus Park, 13, 14, 50
Grant, Ulysses S., *Victory Eagle and
  Pylons* (Fredericks), 42
Graves, Oscar: *Martin Luther King,
  Jr.*, 137
Greater Corktown Development
  Corporation, xv, 132, 134, 135
Gropper, William: *Automotive Mural*,
  87
Grosse Pointe Public Library, 126
Guido, Jeff, 62
Guyton, Karen, 122
Guyton, Tyree: *Heidelberg Project*,
  122–23; *Invisible Doors*, 123

H. Irving Mayson Neighborhood
  Center, 129
Haass, Ernest W. Memorial (Keck),
  140
Hall, Michael D., 72, 204; *Amaranth*,
  204, 213; *Covington*, 213; *Drifter*,
  211, 212; *Stargazer (for Columbus
  Cain)*, 212, 213
Hamilton, Edward N., 36
Hamtramck, 128, 129
Hamtramck Public Library, 129
*The Hand of God, Memorial to Frank
  Murphy* (Milles), 20
Hard Edge Soft Edge (Stiebel), 19
Harley, Ellington, and Day
  (Harley, Ellington, Pierce, Yee
  Associates), 39, 42
Harmonie Park: *The Entrance*
  (Piet), 18; *Hard Edge, Soft Edge*
  (Stiebel), 19
Harris, Carole, 62
Hart, Philip A., Civic Center Plaza,
  xv, 30, 31
Head (Ayrton), xvii
Healy, Ann, 62
Heidelberg Project (Guyton), 122–23
Helios Trail (White), 85
Henry Ford (Fredericks), 156
Hepworth, Barbara, 70
Hermelin, David and Doreen, 211
Hernmarck, Helena, 187
The Hiker (Newman), 116
Hill, Joe, 35
Hip and Spine (Stone Chair Setting)
  (Nonas), 72–73
History of Poland (Orlowski), 129
HMS Products Company, Troy, 196
Hnizdovsky, Jacques, 188
Holbrook Café, Hamtramck, 128,
  129
Holm, Gregory: *Funnel Project* (with
  Randall and Newbold), 134
Hubbard, Bela, 82
Hubbard, Orville, 168
Huffines, Jason, 135
Humoresque (Frishmuth), 198, 214–15
Hunt, Richard, 62

In Honor of Mary Chase Stratton (Pancioli), 52, 64
Internal Revenue Service, 76
International Memorial to the Underground Railroad (Dwight), 31–32
International Theatre Olympiad, 18
International Underground Railroad Monument Collaborative of Detroit, 31
Invisible Doors (Guyton), 123
Italian Tribune of America, 27

James J. Brady Memorial (Cashwan and O'Dell), 9, 117
Jayne, Ira W., 20
Jefferson, Thomas, Mount Rushmore, 43
Jennifer's Butterfly (Scarff), 96–97
Jeune fille et sa suite (Young Woman and Her Suitors) (Calder), 68–69, 217
Joe Louis Arena station, Detroit People Mover, 55
John and Arthur Scott and Company, 26
John Paul II, Pope, 129
John Paul II, Pope (Varga), 128
Johnson, Lester, 62
Jonah and the Whale (Milles), 202
Josephine F. Ford Sculpture Garden, Detroit Cultural Center, xvii, 72, 74, 213
Joyce, James: *Finnegan's Wake*, 67
Jungwirth, Leonard D.: *Father Gabriel Richard*, 110

Kadaj, Lila, 147
Kamrowski, Gerome, 52, 186; *Voyage*, 54
Kaneko, Jun, 52, 53, 186
Katz, Ray: *Burst*, 176–77
Kearney, John: *Silverbolt (Detroit Horse Power IV)*, 94–95
Keck, Charles: *Ernest W. Haass Memorial*, 140
Kern, Father Clement (Chesney), 133
Kidd, Robert, 62

King, Martin Luther, Jr., 135
King, Martin Luther, Jr. (Graves), 137
King, William, 62
Kipp, Lyman: *Salute to Knowledge*, 126
Knodel, Gerhardt: *The Echo of Flora Exotica*, 188–89; *Lifelines*, 188
Kopernik, Mikolaj (Nicolaus Copernicus) (Varga), 78, 80
Korab, Balthazar, 62
Kosciuszko, General Thaddeus (Marconi), 45
Kozloff, Joyce, 52
Kramer, Michaele Duffy: *The Wyandots—A Family Tribute*, 152–53
Kramp, Gretchen, 182
Kuemmerlein, Janet, 62
Kulak, Gary, xvi; *County Seat*, 169–70

Lahti, Taru, 135
Lakeside Shopping Mall, Sterling Heights, 174
LaSalle, Cadillac, Marquette, and Richard (Melchers), 82–83
Laura Sies Memorial (Sestok), 150
Lawrence Technological University, Southfield, 211
Lawson, George A.: *Burns, Robert*, 58, 59
Lawton, James L.: *Pink Landscape—Three Trusses Plus*, 59
Lear Industries, 6
Lehr, Barry: *Ascension*, 139
Leiserowitz, Mel, 125; *City of Southfield*, 210
Leland, Henry N., 8
Lemberg Gallery, 181
Lichtenstein, Roy, 155
Lifelines (Knodel), 188
Linburg, Susanna, 106; *Arch: Montrose*, 77
Lincoln, Abraham: Mount Rushmore, 43; *Victory Eagle and Pylons*, 42
Lincoln, Abraham (Borglum), 43
Lincoln, Abraham (Pelzer), 8
Linton, Harold, 186

Lippold, Richard, xvii
Livonia Civic Center, 160–61
Los Galanes Restaurant, 144
Louis, Joe, Memorial to (Graham), 36–37
Loving, Alan, Jr., 52; *Detroit New Morning*, 54
Lowery, Jayson D.: *Continuity*, 86
Luchs, Michael, 150
Lucifer Landing (Nonas), 73
Ludington Plaza, Wayne State University, 82–83
Luther, Martin (Rietschel), 173
Luther Memorial Park Association, 173

Mackey, Sam, 122
Macomb, General Alexander, xiv
Macomb, General Alexander (Varga), 78
Macomb, General Alexander (Weinman), 50
Macomb County, map of, 162
Macomb County Building, Mt. Clemens, 170
Macomb County Community College, The Commons, South Campus, 166, 167
Macomb County Court Building, Mt. Clemens, 50
Magsig, Steven, 186
Manoogian Endowment for Wildlife Art and Interpretation, 182
Manzu, Giacomo: *Nymph and Faun*, 40, 91–92; *Passo di danza (Dance Step)*, xvi, 40, 91
Marconi, Leonard: *General Thaddeus Kosciuszko*, 45
Marini, Marino, 94, 125
Marquette, LaSalle, Cadillac, and Richard (Melchers), 82–83
Martin Luther King Jr. Memorial Park, 137
Marygrove College, 141
Mason, Stevens T. (Weinert), xiv, 3, 9, 10
Masons, 28
Massey, Hubert: *Kevin C. Flaherty Memorial*, 46–47; *Patterns of Detroit* Community Mural Project (with various artists), 47, 75–76
Matzen, Herman: *Johann Friedrich von Schiller*, 119
Maybury, William C., Elementary School, 147
Maybury, William Cotter Monument (Weinman), 12, 13, 50
McCarthy, John Gregory, 104; *Untitled*, 103
McDonald Square Condominiums, 106
McGee, Charles, 52, 62; *The Blue Nile*, 53; "Noah's Ark" series, 190; *Progression*, 190–91
McGhee, Allie, 52
McGillis, Michael, 147
McGregor Memorial Sculpture Garden, Gullen Mall, Wayne State University, 91–92
McKenzie, Robert Tait: *Boy Scout*, 136
Meadmore, Clement: *Upcast*, 207
Meadows, Gene, 186
Melchers, Julius, xiv, 110, 119; *Marquette, LaSalle, Cadillac, and Richard*, 82–83
Memorial to Joe Louis (Graham), 36–37
Mermaid (Bennett), 121
Merrill Fountain, 139
Mexicantown, xvi, 145–46
Michael Berry International Terminal, Detroit Metropolitan Airport, 44
Michaels, Glen, 52, 62; *Ribbon Fall*, 186
Michigan Avenue station, Detroit People Mover, 54
Michigan Central Station, 134
Michigan Garden (Fletcher), 187
Michigan Labor Legacy Project, 33
Michigan Soldiers and Sailors Monument (Rogers), 3, 4–5, 107
Midmien (Soffer), 90
Mien (Soffer), 90

Millender Center Station, Detroit
People Mover, 54
Millennium Bell (Blake and Turner),
15
Milles, Carl, xiv, 38; *Europa and the
Bull*, 200–201, 202; *Europa
Fountain*, 201; *The Hand of
God, Memorial to Frank Murphy*,
20; *Jonah and the Whale*, 202;
Orpheus Fountain, 202, 203;
Sunglitter, 198–99
Minimalism, 207
Monroe Monument Marker (Babcock
and Ernstberger), 6
Moore, Henry, 70
Mt. Clemens, 169–70, 171–72
Mt. Clemens Art in Public Places, 169
Mt. Clemens Public Library, 186
Mt. Elliott Cemetery, 108
Mural (Ferretti), 132, 135
*Murphy, Frank, Memorial to, The
Hand of God* (Milles), 20
Murray, Robert: *Nordkyn*, 93
Museum of African American
History. *See* Charles H. Wright
Museum of African American
History

Nakian, Reuben, 72
Nani, James: *Renaissance Rebirth*, 105
Nardin Park, 137
National Institute for the
Conservation of Cultural
Property, xvii
National Museum of American Art
(Smithsonian Institution), xvii
Neiman Marcus, xvi, 193
Nelson, Sabrina, 76
Nevelson, Louise, xiv; *Trilogy*, 60–61
Newbold, Abigail: *Funnel Project*
(with Randall and Holm), 134
New Center One, 96–97, 150
New Detroit, Inc., xv, 19
Newman, Allen G.: *The Hiker*, 116;
Spanish American War Monument,
116
Newman, Kirk, 52, 62; *On the Move*,
54

Newton, Gordon, 150
"Noah's Ark" series (McGee), 190
Nobili, Louise, 62
Noguchi, Isamu, xiv, xv; *Dodge,
Horace E., and Son Memorial
Fountain*, 30; *Pylon*, 5, 29
Nonas, Richard, 204; *Hip and Spine
(Stone Chair Setting)*, 72–73;
Lucifer Landing, 73
Nordkyn (Murray), 93
Normanno Wedge I (Pepper), 74
North Corktown, 135
Nymph and Faun (Manzu), 40, 91–92

Oakland County, map of, 178
Object Orange, 181
O'Dell, Frederick C.: *James J. Brady
Memorial* (with Cashwan), 9, 117
Olbrot, Andrzej W., 84
Oldenburg, Claes, 155
Old Newsboys Goodfellows of
Detroit, 117
One Woodward Plaza Building, xvi,
40
Ono, Yoko: *Wish Tree for Detroit*, 49
On the Move (Newman), 54
Orchestra Place Courtyard, 60–61
Orlowski, Dennis, 76; *History of
Poland*, 128, 129
Orpheus Fountain (Milles), 202, 203
Osip, Sandra: *Progression II*, 52, 55

Pallas, Jim, 182
Palmer Park, 139
Pancioli, Diana: *Arc*, 63–64; *In Honor
of Mary Chase Stratton*, 52, 64
Pangus, Craig, 195
Pappas, John Nick: *The Procession (A
Family)*, 24–25, 152
Parducci, Corrado Joseph: *Horace
H. Rackham Memorial Fountain*
(with Schnaple), 182
Parks, Rosa, 135
Parks, Rosa Transit Center, 49
Parks, Valerie, 62
Park Shelton Apartments, xvii
Parkview Square apartments, 105
Passo di danza (Dance Step) (Manzu),

40, 91

Patterns of Detroit Community Mural Project (Massey and various artists), 47, 75–76

Peck Park, 75, 76

Pelzer, Alfonso: *Abraham Lincoln*, 8; *Law, Commerce, Agriculture, and Mechanics*, 8, 26

Penelopeia (Court), 142–43

Penobscot Building, 132

People around the Universe: Our Green Land and Blue Water (Kadaj et al.), 148

People Mover stations, Art in, xvi, 47, 52–55

Pepper, Beverly, 72; *Normanno Wedge I*, 74

Perez, Hector, 147

Perry, Commodore Oliver Hazard, *Victory Eagle and Pylons* (Fredericks), 42

Pewabic Pottery, 52, 63–64, 112

Phardel, Tom, 52, 76

Philip A. Hart Civic Center Plaza, xv, 30, 31

Phoenix (Veresh), 70

Piet, John: *ABZ—Everything Is Anything*, 124; *The Carnival!* 102; *The Entrance*, 18

Pingree, Hazen S., xiv

Pingree, Hazen S. Memorial (Schwarz), 12, 13

Pingree Park, 18, 124

Pink Landscape—Three Trusses Plus (Lawton), 59

Polish American Century Club, 129

Pollack, Alexander: *Eastern Market Murals*, 127

Pontiac, Chief, *Victory Eagle and Pylons* (Fredericks), 42

Pop Art movement, 155

Pope Park, Hamtramck, 128

Portman, John, 29

Price, Dr. Glenda D., 141

The Procession (A Family) (Pappas), 24–25

Progression II (Osip), 55

Progression (McGee), 190–91

Public Art Project, 181

Pulaski, Count Casimir (Dunikowski), 151

Pulaski, General Casimir, 45, 78

Pulaski Park, 151

Puntigam, Jim: *The Corn Field* (with Valdez), 145–46

Pylon (Noguchi), 5, 29

Rackham, Horace H., 66, 182

Rackham, Horace H. Memorial Fountain (Parducci), xv, 182

Rackham, Mary, 182

Randall, Samantha: *Funnel Project* (with Holm and Newbold), 134

Rashid, Kathleen, 76

Redstone, Louis G., 44, 125

Reflective Head (Ayrton), 194–95

Release (Rost et al.), 147, 148

Renaissance Center. *See* General Motors World Headquarters

Renaissance Rebirth (Nani), 105

Reuther, Walter P., 20

Revolution, 181

Rhind, John Massey: *Victory and Progress*, 26

Rhythms and Vibrations (Stiebel), 19

Ribbon Fall (Michaels), 186

Richard, Father Gabriel, *Victory Eagle and Pylons* (Fredericks), 42

Richard, Father Gabriel (Jungwirth), 110

Richard, LaSalle, Cadillac, and Marquette (Melchers), 82–83

Richard and Jane Manoogian Endowment for Wildlife Art and Interpretation, 182

Rietschel, Ernst F. A.: *Martin Luther*, 173

Rivalta, Augusto: *Christopher Columbus*, 27

Rivera, Diego: *Detroit Industry* frescos, 87

The River of Knowledge (Sheets), 79, 81

Robinson, Phaedra, 181

Rodin, Auguste, 43; *The Thinker*, 66

231

Rogers, Randolph: *Michigan Soldiers and Sailors Monument*, 3, 4–5, 107; *Waterman Monument (Flight of the Spirit)*, 107

Romanelli, Raffaello: *Dante Alighieri*, 119, 120

Roosevelt, Theodore: Mount Rushmore, 43; *Victory Eagle and Pylons* (Fredericks), 42

Rosa Parks Transit Center, 49

The Rosebuds (Trimpe), 168

Roseland Park Cemetery, 185

Rosenthal, Bernard (Tony): *Cranbrook Ingathering*, 204; *T-Square*, 204

Roseville City Hall, 168

Rost, Steven, 147

Royal Oak, 182, 183, 186, 187, 188–89, 190–91, 192

Royal Oak City Hall, Barbara Hallman Plaza, 183

Rubello, David: *Color Cubes*, 51

Rudd, Tom, 135

Rushmore, Mount, 43

Rutzky, Ivy Sky: *Glacial*, 167

Saarinen, Eero, 165

Saarinen, Eliel, 201

Saint-Gaudens, Augustus, 13, 14, 50, 118, 140

Salute to Knowledge (Kipp), 126

Scarab Club, 70

Scarff, S. Thomas: *An American Lightbow*, 96–97; *Jennifer's Butterfly*, 96–97

Scarlett, Linda, 52

Schefman, Robert, 62

Schiller, Johann Friedrich von (Matzen), 119

Schnaple, Frederick A.: *Horace H. Rackham Memorial Fountain* (with Parducci), 182

Schneider, Arthur: *Untitled*, 125

Schwarz, Rudolph: *Hazen S. Pingree Memorial*, 12, 13

Scott, James Memorial Fountain (Gilbert and Adams), xv, 111–12

Scott, John and Arthur, and Company, 26

Scott, Walter, 58

Sekhaoelo, Solomon, 62

Sentinel II (Brose), 10

Sentinel X (Brose), 10, 11

Sentry (Bennett), 65

Serra, Richard, 72

Sestok, Robert: *Continuity Tower*, 98–99, 150; *Dancing Hands*, 21–22, 150; *Laura Sies Memorial*, 150, 197; *Untitled*, 150

Shain Park, Birmingham, 208–9

Sheets, Millard: *The River of Knowledge*, 79

Shrady, Henry Merwin: *Major General Alpheus Starkey Williams*, 118

Sies, Laura Memorial (Sestok), 197

Silverbolt (Detroit Horse Power IV) (Kearney), 94–95

Silverman, Lila and Gilbert B., xv, 49, 90, 213

Sister Earth (Contreras), 109

Sister Moon (Frankel), 109

Sister Water (Tawil), 109

Six-Tonner for Julian (Beasley), 174

Slows Bar BQ Restaurant, 134

Smith, Alice, 135

Smith, Ann F.: *The Dance of Life*, 106

Smith, G. Alden: *Wings of Learning*, 88

Smith, Tony, 207; *Gracehoper*, 67

Snowden, Gilda, 76

Soffer, Sasson: *Midmien*, 90; *Mien*, 90

Solanus Casey Center, 109

Soldiers and Sailors Monument, 6

SOS! (Save Outdoor Sculpture!), xvii

Sousanis, Nick, 181

Southfield, 210, 211, 212

Southfield Civic Center, 210

Spanish American War Monument (Newman), 116

The Spirit of Detroit (Fredericks), xiv, 38–39

The Spirit of Sterling Heights (Wood), 175, 176

Spirit of the American Doughboy (Visquesney), 184–85

Standing Together (Wood), 175

Star Dream (Fredericks), 183

Stargazer (for Columbus Cain) (Hall), 212

Steel V (Stoltz), 104

Sterling Heights Civic Center, xvi, 141, 175, 176–77

Sticker Woman (Surls), 193

Stiebel, Hanna: *Hard Edge Soft Edge*, 19; *Rhythms and Vibrations*, 19

Stoltz, David, 103; *Carousel*, 104; *Fanfare*, 104; *Steel V*, 104

Stonerov, Oscar, 106

Storm, James: *Galileo's Night Vision* (with Wesner), 171–72

Stratton, Mary Chase, In Honor of (Pancioli), 52, 64

Stratton, Mary Chase Perry, 182

Stroh Brewery Company, 64

Sugarman, George, 62

Sunglitter (Milles), 198–99

Surls, James: *Sticker Woman*, xvi, 193

Sykes, Ed: *Untitled*, 84

"Symbol Wall," *The Spirit of Detroit* (Fredericks), 38

Taubman Company, Inc., 174

Tawil, Hashim al-: *Sister Water*, 109

Tchakmakchian, Arto: *Gomidas*, 41

Teicher, Lois: benches, Boll Family YMCA, xvi; *Curved Form with Rectangle and Space*, 70–71

Thayer, Russell: *Untitled*, 157

The Thinker (Rodin), 66

Times Square/Robert L. Hurst Jr. Park, 49

Timlin, Hugh: *Covenant*, 108

Ting, Vassely, 62

Tobin, Farley, 52

Tower of Freedom (Dwight), 31–32

Transcending (De Giusti and Barr), 23, 33–35, 42, 165

Trilogy (Nevelson), 60–61

Trimpe, Janet B.: *The Rosebuds*, 168

Triton Pool, 201

Troy, 193, 194–95, 196

Truth, Sojourner, 5

T-Square (Rosenthal), 204

Turner, Christopher: *Millennium Bell*, 15

Type "A" Personality (Beltchenko), 141

UAW-Ford Center, 42, 43, 110

Underground Railroad, International Memorial to the (Dwight), 31–32

Underground Railroad Monument Committee of Windsor, 31

Uniroyal Tire (Big Tire), 154–55

Untitled (Arman), 158

Untitled (Byars), 159

Untitled (Dolega), 113

Untitled (McCarthy), 103

Untitled (Schneider), 125

Untitled (Sestok), 150

Untitled (Sykes), 84

Untitled (Thayer), 157

Untitled (Whyte), 135

Untitled (Youngman), 44

Upcast (Meadmore), 207

Urban Stele (De Giusti), 22–23

Valdez, Vito, 76; *Big Fish*, 145; *The Corn Field* (with Puntigam), 145–46

Vandervennet, Robert, 143

Varga, Ferenc, 133, 153; *John Paul II, Pope*, 178; *Mikolaj Kopernik (Nicolaus Copernicus)*, 78, 80; monument to Pulaski, 151

Varga, Frank, statue of General Alexander Macomb, 50, 78, 169

Vartabed, Father Gomidas, 41

Veresh, Steve: *Phoenix*, 70

Veterans Memorial Building. *See* UAW-Ford Center

Victor Emmanuel II, Rome, 27

Victory Eagle and Pylons (Fredericks), 42

Victory and Progress (Rhind), xiv, 26

Vihos, George, 62, 186

Visquesney, Ernest M.: *Spirit of the American Doughboy*, 184–85

"Voices of Labor" plinth, *Transcending* (Barr and De Giusti), 35

Voulkos, Peter, 204

Voyage (Kamrowski), 54

Wagner, Edward, 26
Wagstaff, Samuel J., Jr., 67
Walesa, Lech, 129
Ward, Jack, 217
Warhol, Andy, 155
Warren, 164–65, 166, 167
Warren Civic Center, 164–65
Washington, George, Mount Rushmore, 43
Washington, George (DeLue), 28
Waterman, J. W., 107
Waterman Monument (Flight of the Spirit) (Rogers), 107
Wave Composition (Gilliam), 62, 63
Waves (Bennett), 121
Wayne, General Anthony, Wayne County Building, 26
Wayne, General Anthony (De Giusti), 23, 89
Wayne County Building: General Anthony Wayne, 26; *Law, Commerce, Agriculture, and Mechanics*, 8, 26; *Victory and Progress*, xiv
Wayne State University: Anthony Wayne Drive and West Warren Avenue, 84; Centennial Courtyard, 89; College of Engineering, 85; Community Arts Building, Reuther Mall, 90; Ferry Mall, 93; Gullen Mall, 86; Ludington Plaza, 82–83; McGregor Memorial Sculpture Garden, Gullen Mall, 91–92; Mort Harris Recreation and Fitness Center, Gullen Mall, 88; Student Center Building, Gullen Mall, 87; Welcome Center, 123
Webber Memorial Building, Grace Hospital, 44
Weinert, Albert: *Mason, Stevens T.*, 9
Weinman, Adolph Alexander: *General Alexander Macomb* memorial, 12, 13, 50; *William Cotter Maybury Monument*, 12, 13, 50
Wesner, Joseph: *Galileo's Night Vision* (with Storm), 171–72
West and South Detroit, map of, 130

Western International High School, 147
Whale Tower (Wyland), 16, 17
Wheaton, Marilyn L., 15
White, Bruce: *Helios Trail*, 85
Whyte, Graem: *Untitled*, 135
William Beaumont Hospital, Royal Oak, xv, 53, 143, 186, 187, 188, 190–91, 192
William C. Maybury Elementary School, 147
Williams, Major General Alpheus Starkey (Shrady), xiv, 118
Wings of Learning (Smith), 88
A Wish for Peace (Perez et al.), 148, 149
Wish Tree for Detroit (Ono), 49
Wolfgang, Myra, 35
Wood, Marcia: *The Spirit of Sterling Heights*, 175, 176; *Standing Together*, 175
Woodlawn Cemetery, xiv, 140
Woodman, George, 52
Woodward Monument Marker (Babcock and Ernstberger), 3, 6
Works Progress Administration Federal Arts Project, 110
"World's Largest Stove," 155
Wright, Charles H. Museum of African American History. *See* Charles H. Wright Museum of African American History
Wright, Frank Lloyd, 67
The Wyandots—A Family Tribute (Kramer), 152–53
Wyandotte, 151, 152–53
Wyandotte Street Art Fair, 152
Wyland, Robert: *Whale Tower*, 16, 17

The X and Its Tails (Calder), 69

Yamasaki, Minoru, 40, 91
Youngman, W. Robert, 125; *Untitled*, 44

Zeiger, Allen, 214
Zox, Larry, 186